WOODCARVING ILLUSTRATED
Book 2

D1604649

DATE DUE

WOODCARVING ILLUSTRATED
Book 2

**8 Useful Projects
You Can Make out of Wood**

Paul McCarthy, *1942 –*

and

Roger Schroeder

Stackpole Books

Copyright © 1985 by Stackpole Books
Published by
STACKPOLE BOOKS
Cameron and Kelker Streets
P.O. Box 1831
Harrisburg, PA 17105

Cover photograph by Tad Goodale.
Photographs in this book, unless otherwise credited,
are by Roger Schroeder.

Printed in the U.S.A.

Library of Congress Cataloging-in-Publication Data

McCarthy, Paul, 1942–
    Woodcarving illustrated, book 2.

    1. Wood-carving—Technique.   I. Schroeder,
Roger, 1945–   .   II. Title.   III. Title:
Woodcarving illustrated, book two.
NK9704.M44   1985   736'.4   85-10081
ISBN 0-8117-2285-6

to Wendy McCarthy
and
to Armand LaMontagne

Contents

PART ONE

Materials and Techniques for Woodcarving

1

Introduction

Based on the success of *Woodcarving Illustrated*, it seemed inevitable that Book 2 would be published with eight brand new projects for the beginning and intermediate carver.

When Paul and I got together to do that first book, we decided that wood-carving could be better illustrated than photographed. But more important, we wanted to offer illustrations that brought the reader from the very beginning of the project to its completion, with no tool cut left to the reader's imagination. So when you open another book and discover only four line drawings describing how a piece is carved, close it. Open ours, and find as many as forty or more finely done illustrations for a single project.

The eight projects in *Woodcarving Illustrated Book 2* are perhaps a bit more challenging than those in the previous book. In fact, we start you off with a mirror that could be considered two projects. The rope frame is one; the sailing ship on top of the frame is another. They can be carved as separate gift items, or made jointly, as they are in this book.

We also offer such decorative pieces as a traditional eagle, a half ship's hull, a rainbow trout, a mallard decoy, and a rose wall plaque. This last one

I find particularly intriguing. It's a study in low relief carving that can be transferred to door panels, furniture, and other wall plaques.

The wall clock is another fascinating project. More than a useful time-piece, it is also a learning experience in perspective carving. Once you master this technique, you will be able to carve in low relief any building – even your own house.

Another project is a chess and checkers board. It's not just a slab of wood with lines carved into it. With its four carved legs, this game board will be the talk of the neighborhood, or the carving club you might belong to.

Is there an order to these projects? There is and there isn't. Perhaps one of the hardest comes first. But this project – the nautical wall mirror – introduces you to the McCarthy knife, developed by Paul; to the fishtail that can remove background wood; and to a V parting tool that can define lines. It's a project that will lead you to more wood removal and in-the-round figures, such as the mallard decoy. There's also a project that employs basically flat, or incised, cuts. This is the wall clock with its clock-face pointers and light-house buildings.

What we have, then, is a balance of practical and decorative carvings to be enjoyed yourself or given to friends. Also, we keep the number of tools to a minimum, with four or five taking care of nearly all the cuts. A listing of appropriate tools appears on the first illustrated page of each project.

We limit even the wood to two popular species: white pine and basswood. Both are easily obtained at local lumberyards. But if you can't find the right wood, you might want to write to co-author Paul McCarthy. He'll send you wooden blanks sawn to shape. Take a look at chapter 5, "Where to Find Supplies," for his address. In that same chapter, you'll also find out where to buy the tools used throughout our book.

I might point out that many writers of carving books repeat the same introductory material on tools and woods and sharpening and finishing in book after book. Paul and I decided not to do that. In Book 2, we've shortened the text considerably, devoting more pages to the projects. What we do have in the beginning is new material, with helpful hints on glues and gluing up, making a compass, and how Paul's "McCarthy knife" can be used for many of the projects. In our first book, you'll find all you need to know about basic tools and how to keep them sharp, which woods work and which ones don't, and how to finish that piece you spent so many hours carving.

But before I let you go on to the next few chapters, you should learn

Co-author Paul McCarthy.

Co-author Roger Schroeder.

something about our backgrounds. I think the best way to describe them is to say that they are "wood intensive."

Aside from being a fine teacher of carving students at his shop in Scituate Harbor, Massachusetts, Paul McCarthy is one of the finest and most sought-after sign carvers in the country. With their incised, gold-leafed letters and imaginative motifs, his signs are the pride of many businesses and private homes throughout New England and other parts of the country.

How did I meet Paul? I interviewed him for an article I was writing for *Fine Woodworking* magazine back in 1979. (You can read more about Paul in issue No. 30.) Besides *Woodcarving Illustrated*, I've written two other books for Stackpole, *How to Carve Wildfowl* and *Waterfowl Carving with J. D. Sprankle*.

And I've been doing cabinetwork for over fifteen years, combining fine joinery with carving to produce carved pieces of furniture.

Enjoy the projects as much as we enjoyed writing about them, and please read our first book. It starts the story of how woodcarving, provided there are good text and drawings, is within the reach of almost anyone.

Roger Schroeder
Amityville, New York

2

The McCarthy Knife

History of the Knife

Co-author Paul McCarthy had been incising his hand-lettered signs for years, using what has been called a Murphy, or mill, knife. The distinctive feature of this tool is a long blade that slides through a wooden handle of wood and brass. But experimenting with it, and changing the shape of the skewed angle of the cutting edge, McCarthy came up with a fixed-blade knife. With it, he can not only do lettering but also remove wood from backgrounds and even do figures.

His knife is made from high speed steel, ground and honed for immediate use. The handle is usually walnut and coated with linseed oil. The blade is easily maintained by honing it on a soft or hard Arkansas stone, or equivalent Japanese water stone. (For more on sharpening and stones, refer to *Woodcarving Illustrated*.) To purchase this custom-made knife, see chapter 5.

It's a versatile knife that allows Paul or any other carver to get close enough to his work to control the cuts, while drawing the knife toward him or pushing it away.

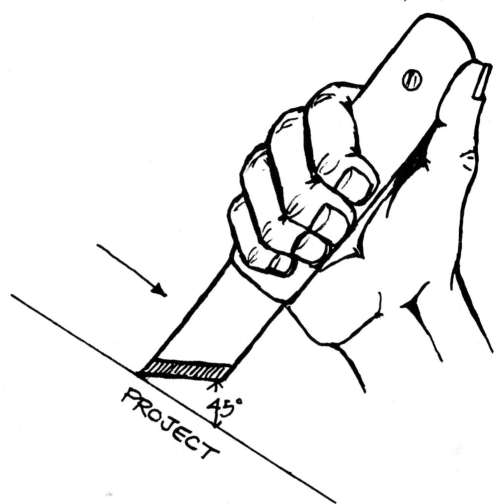

The draw method using the McCarthy knife.

The Draw Method

Many projects, especially low relief carvings, require straight-down or stop cuts when cutting around an object or down into an incised letter. To use the McCarthy knife when drawing the tool toward you, grasp it firmly and place your little finger as near as possible to the end of the handle where it joins the blade. But you don't want that finger around the blade. Place your thumb firmly against the back edge of the handle and draw the point of the blade through the wood. While pushing with your thumb and pulling with

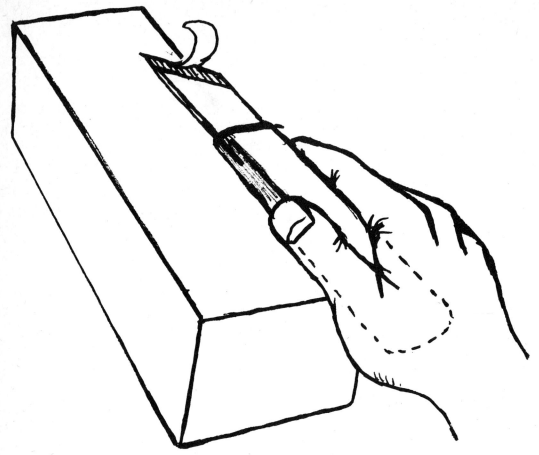

The push method using the McCarthy knife.

the rest of your fingers, you should be able to maintain the angle of the blade to your project.

The Push Method

Not all cuts with the McCarthy knife or any tool like it require pulling the tool toward you. Many wood removal cuts require that you push the tool *away* from you. This is especially useful when rounding or hollowing.

McCarthy had experimented with a traditional skew chisel, but found that the blade was too long to have enough control over the cuts. So he retained the skew cut blade for his knife and shortened the blade considerably. McCarthy finds his knife ideal for slicing away wood, even hardwood.

He says that pushing off wood quickly is like cutting meat. You don't push the blade into it, you slice *through* it. To use the knife, then, for pushing, grasp it firmly in the palm of your hand with your thumb on the top edge of the handle and your fingers pressing the handle into the palm. Holding the knife this way, you will be able to lay it very flat to the work to achieve rounding or even hollowing without digging into the wood. You can remove as much or as little as you want simply by adjusting the angle of the blade as you raise or lower your hand.

3

Gluing Up

At least two of the projects will require that you join boards together to make a single piece of wood or panel. Since it is often hard to get wood in widths big enough to accommodate patterns, gluing two or more boards together is usually necessary. This is the case for the mirror, which requires wood 16 inches wide, and the clock, which requires wood 14 inches wide. But even if you did find a single board large enough, the chances of it warping or curving along its width are great.

When you are gluing together flat boards, a good rule of thumb is not to exceed 8 inches in board width for ¾-inch-thick stock or 10 inches in width for 2-inch-thick wood. For both the mirror and clock, you can use two boards.

Pipe clamps are probably the best kind of clamp to use, since they will lie flat on the floor or workbench without tipping to one side. Also, they are fairly inexpensive, though you will have to buy the clamping jaws and plumber's pipes separately. But they can be coupled together to achieve indefinitely long lengths.

The best procedure for clamping wood edge to edge is to get the clamps

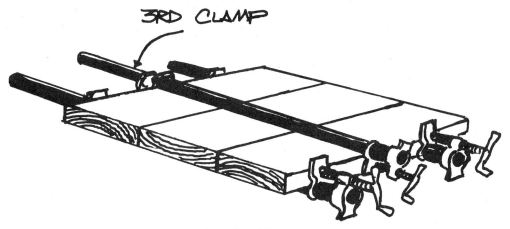

Joining boards with pipe clamps.

underneath and above the boards. If you used clamps only underneath and none on top, the wood would buckle or bow. A top clamp or clamps prevent this and also allow for even drying of the glue.

After you've given the boards' edges an even coating of glue, lay them down and line up their ends so they are not staggered. Apply a little pressure with the bottom clamps until some glue starts to squeeze out at the seams. Place at least one clamp on the top of the panel and apply about the same pressure on it as you did on the bottom clamps.

How many clamps should you use? If the wood is pine and only 2 or 3 feet long, two on the bottom and one on the top are probably sufficient. A longer panel and harder wood will require more clamps.

Also, keep the ends of all the clamps on the same side. This way, you don't have to jump from one side to the other to tighten them. And it takes up less room, especially if the pipe clamps are long ones.

Is the oozing-out glue a problem? Not if you put newspaper underneath the clamps and beyond them. Even the glue itself is not a problem if you allow it to dry. It is much easier to remove the beads when hard with a chisel than when wet with a rag. That glue will seep into the pores of the wood and prevent stain from penetrating.

Applying glue to boards to be joined.

Glues

There are many types of glues to use when putting boards together, but which one you use depends on what you are gluing and where the project is going to end up. Simply put, you should buy brands such as Titebond or Elmer's Carpenter's Wood Glue for interior work. For exterior projects, waterproof or a resorcinol or epoxy glue is needed. Both are two-part glues.

Whichever you use, lay out your boards on the pipe clamps, lift up two at a time, and run a thick bead of the glue along the edges. To add a little more strength to the bond, we recommend that you score or scratch those edges with a knife or other sharp instrument. A linoleum knife is ideal because of its hooked blade.

Yet another trick is to glue the boards so that their end grains alternate. This means that one board has its grain curving one way whereas the adjacent board has its grain running the other way. This keeps the boards from warping all in the same direction and thereby forming a large concave or convex surface.

With the interior glues such as the Elmer's Carpenter's Wood Glue, you can get a tight bond in at least an hour. With waterproof glues such as the resorcinol, you need a longer drying time. But whichever you use, it's best to save the gluing as the last thing to be done for the day so that the glue has a chance to dry overnight.

4

Making a Compass

For the mirror frame and the dial face of the clock, you will need a compass, a tool for drawing circles. Probably the simplest of all methods for making circles is a pencil tied to a piece of string and held vertically to the surface. But this method is frustrating because it is difficult to keep the pencil straight up and down and to keep the proper tension on the string. Also, if you change the required 90-degree angle of the pencil to the circle, the line will not meet where it began.

Instead, you can make a compass, one that will take some work, but a tool you can keep permanently. And it can be made in nine easy steps.

Step 1. Select two pieces of wood that measure ¾ inches x ¾ inches x 18 inches. The type of wood doesn't matter though a hardwood like maple will take abuse and last nearly forever. See fig. 1.

Step 2. With a bandsaw or a carving tool such as a fishtail gouge used for many of the projects, remove a piece of wood ¼ inch x 1½ inches from both sides of parallels A and B. See figs. 1 and 2.

Step 3. Next, drill a ⅜-inch-diameter hole through both parallels at the

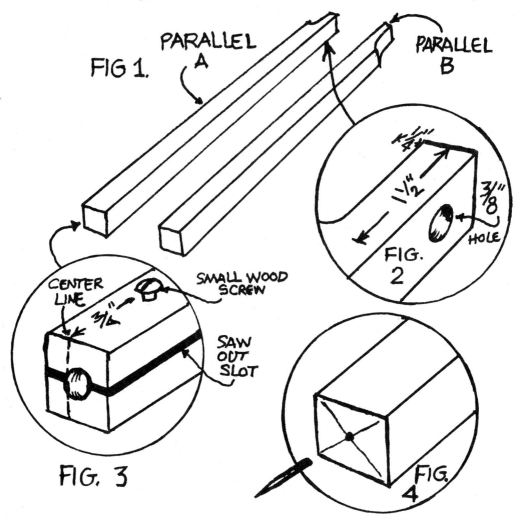

Making a compass, Steps 1–7.

same time while holding them together. This allows both holes to match up perfectly for a bolt. See fig. 2.

Step 4. With a $^{19}/_{64}$-inch drill bit, one very close to the size of the diameter of a standard pencil, drill into the end grain of parallel A. Make the hole deep enough to house a stubby pencil. When drilling this hole, make it a little off center. See fig. 3. Be careful not to drill a crooked hole.

Step 5. Make a saw cut about 2 inches long, splitting in half the hole made in step 4. See fig. 3.

Step 6. Drill a pilot hole for a ⅝-inch wood screw ¾ inches up from the end of parallel A. See fig. 3. This screw will tighten together the halves that hold the pencil and will keep the pencil from eventually slipping out. If you can manage it, drill the hole for the screw so that this hole just touches the hole for the pencil. If this can be done, the screw threads will cut into the side of the pencil and help hold it in place.

Step 7. On the end of parallel B, draw an X from corner to corner to locate the center. Take a 6d finishing nail and cut off its head with a pair of pliers or bolt cutters. Hammer it into parallel B at the center of the X with the point of the head protruding about ⅜ inches. See fig. 4.

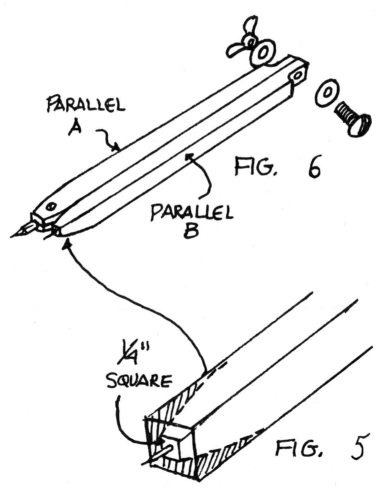

PARALLEL
A

FIG. 6

PARALLEL
B

¼" SQUARE

FIG. 5

Making a compass, Steps 8 and 9.

Step 8. Carve the end of parallel B by gradually tapering it toward the nail. See fig. 5. Leave an area ¼-inch square for the end. Do the same for parallel A, but leave ⅛ inch of wood around the pencil.

Step 9. Obtain a ⅜-inch slotted round head carriage bolt, two steel washers, and a wingnut. Put the bolts through the ⅜-inch holes previously drilled into the tops of the parallels. This arrangement will allow you to adjust the compass by releasing and tightening the wingnut. See fig. 6.

5

Appendix–
Where to Find Supplies

Tools and Wood

Artistry in Veneers, Inc.
450 Oak Tree Avenue
South Plainfield, NJ 07080
201-668-1430

J. Cheaps & Sons
Cheaps Pond Park
Box 7199
Warrensville, OH 44128
800-821-4142

Craftsman Wood Service Company
1735 W. Cortland Court
Addison, IL 60101
312-629-3100

The Fine Tool Shops
P.O. Box 1262
20 Backus Avenue
Danbury, CT 06810
800-243-1037

National Carvers Museum
14960 Woodcarver Road
Monument, CO 80132
303-481-2656

Frank Mittermeier Inc.
3577 East Tremont Avenue
New York, NY 10465
212-823-3843

Shopsmith, Inc.
6640 Poe Avenue
Dayton, OH 45414-2591
800-543-7586

Woodcraft Supply Corp.
41 Atlantic Avenue
Box 4000
Woburn, MA 01888
800-225-1153

The Woodworker's Store
21801 Industrial Boulevard
Rogers, MN 55374
612-428-4101

Woodworker's Supply
5604 Alameda N.E.
Albuquerque, NM
800-645-9292

Clock Parts and Movements

Armor Products
Box 445
East Northport, NY 11731
516-462-6228

Albert Constantine and Son, Inc.
2050 Eastchester Road
Bronx, NY 10461
800-223-8087

Craft Products Company
2200 Dean Street
St. Charles, IL 60174
312-584-9600

Cryder Creek
Box 19
Whitesville, NY 14897
607-356-3303

Elcraft Company
P.O. Box 111
Carlsbad, CA 92008
619-722-2866

Klockit
P.O. Box 629
Highway H North
Lake Geneva, WI 53147
414-248-1150

Mason & Sullivan
586 Higgens Crowel Road
West Yarmouth, Cape Cod, MA 02673
617-778-0475; 778-0477

Garret Wade
161 Avenue of the Americas
New York, NY 10013
800-221-2942

Warren Tool Company
Rt. 1
Box 14AS
Rhinebeck, NY 12572
914-876-7817

Wood Patterns and the McCarthy Knife

Paul McCarthy's Carving Place
132 Front Street
Scituate Harbor, MA 02066

Burning Tools

Annex Manufacturing
955 Blue Ball Road
Elkton, MD 21921

Chesterfield Craft Shop
P.O. Box 208
Chesterfield, NJ 08620

Colwood Electronics
(The Detailer)
715 Westwood Avenue
Long Branch, NJ 07740

Hot Tools, Inc.
7 Hawkes Street
P.O. Box 615
Marblehead, MA 01945

PART TWO

Projects for Woodcarving

Nautical

WALL MIRROR

TOOLS NEEDED · McCARTHY KNIFE
FISHTAIL GOUGE
'V' PARTING TOOL

SHIP PATTERN
(FOR ORNAMENTAL
TOP OF NAUTICAL
MIRROR)

35

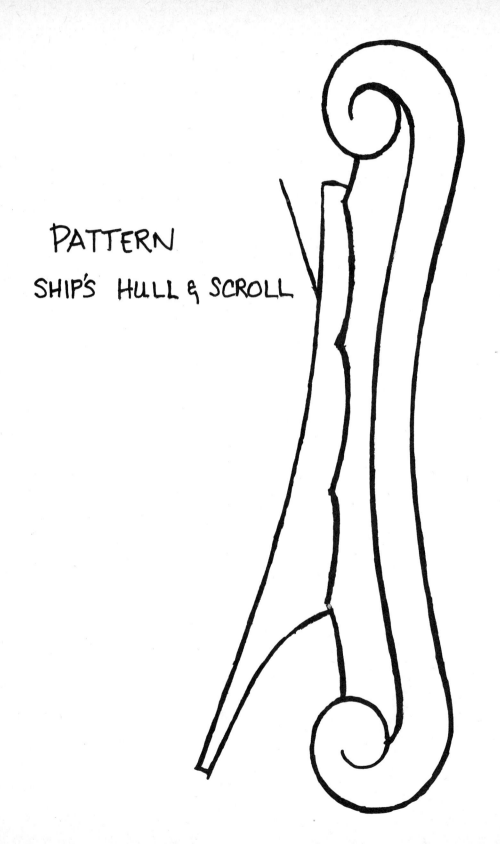

PATTERN

SHIP'S HULL & SCROLL

STEP 1 · STARTING THE MIRROR (TRANSFER PATTERN)
WITH 2 PIECES OF TRACING PAPER, TRACE FROM THE
PATTERN PAGES THE SHIP & THE HULL & SCROLL (FIG. 1).
ALIGN BOTH THESE TRACINGS SO THEY FIT TOGETHER
& MAKE A FULL SIZE PATTERN FOR THE TOP OF YOUR
MIRROR. YOU CAN ALSO MAKE A MORE PERMANENT
PATTERN BY USING POSTER BOARD OR CARDBOARD.

FIG. 1

TRACING
PAPER

STEP 2. USING THE COMPASS

ON A PIECE OF HEAVY PAPER OR CARDBOARD, USE YOUR COMPASS TO DRAW A 16" CIRCLE FOR THE OUTSIDE DIAMETER OF THE MIRROR. DRAW ANOTHER CIRCLE 13" IN DIAMETER FOR THE INSIDE. DRAW TWO ADDITIONAL INNER CIRCLES 1/4" WIDE. MAKE SURE YOU HAVE LEFT ENOUGH ROOM (AT LEAST 10") AT THE TOP OF THE PAPER TO ADD SHIP & SCROLL (FIG. 2) TO MAKE ENTIRE FULL SIZE MIRROR PATTERN.

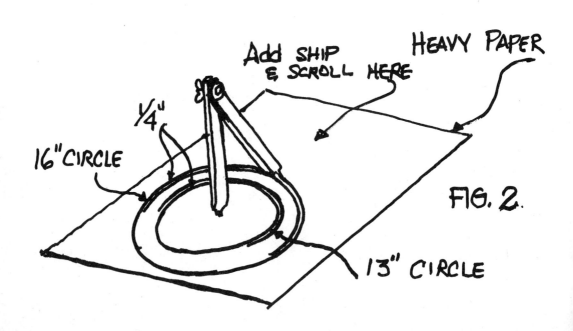

Add SHIP & SCROLL HERE

HEAVY PAPER

1/4"

16" CIRCLE

FIG. 2.

13" CIRCLE

STEP 3 · CUTTING OUT

AFTER THE PATTERN HAS BEEN TRANSFERRED TO THE WOOD, WHICH SHOULD HAVE BEEN MADE FROM AT LEAST TWO BOARDS 2" THICK, EACH ABOUT 8" WIDE & 26" LONG TO ALLOW ROOM TO CUT AWAY WASTE WOOD. IT WOULD BE BEST TO DO THIS WITH A BANDSAW. A JIG SAW WILL ALSO DO THE TRICK, BUT A BANDSAW CUTS CLEANER, LEAVING A STRAIGHTER EDGE. TO CUT INSIDE THE CIRCLE, SAW DIRECTLY INTO BOTTOM OF CIRCLE TO REMOVE WOOD FROM THE INSIDE. TO CLOSE THE CUT, GLUE & CLAMP WITH A BAR CLAMP & PIECES OF THE WASTE WOOD REMOVED FROM OUTER CIRCLE (FIG. 3).

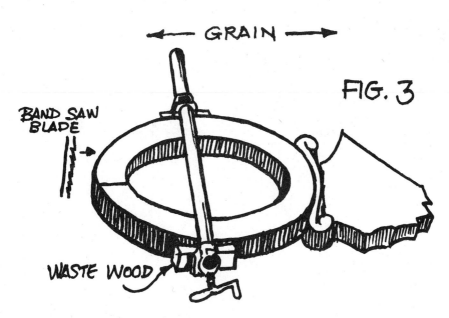

GRAIN

FIG. 3

BAND SAW BLADE

WASTE WOOD

STEP 4 • OUTLINE WITH THE McCARTHY KNIFE

FIGURE 4 SHOWS A SECTION OF THE FRAME FOR THE MIRROR. USING THE DRAW METHOD WITH THE McCARTHY KNIFE, CUT STRAIGHT DOWN & ALONG THE 1/4" INNER CIRCLES & REMOVE WOOD TO A DEPTH OF 3/4". YOU WILL ALSO BE CUTTING IN ALONG THE OUTSIDE DIAMETER OF THE WOOD. A QUICK WAY TO GET A GUIDELINE FOR THAT DEPTH IS TO HOLD A PENCIL IN YOUR FINGERS WITH 3/4" OF THE END PROJECTING BEYOND YOUR FINGERTIPS & RUN YOUR HAND ALONG THE FACE OF THE MIRROR. THE PENCIL LEAD SHOULD LEAVE A FAINT MARK. DO NOT TRY TO CUT THESE PIECES OUT WITH ONE STROKE. AND BE CAREFUL TO KEEP THE KNIFE AT A 90° ANGLE. IF YOU DO NOT, THE SIZE OF THE FINISHED ROPE THAT RUNS ON TOP OF THE INTERIOR OF THE FRAME WILL VARY IN WIDTH.

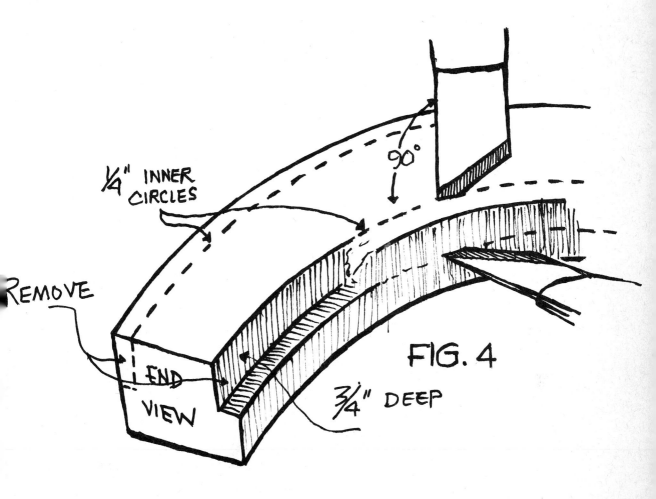

¼" INNER CIRCLES

90°

REMOVE

END VIEW

FIG. 4

¾" DEEP

STEP 5. CUTTING AT AN ANGLE
IT IS DIFFICULT TO CONTINUE THE 1/4" × 3/4" CUT
WHEN YOU GET TO THE SHIP & SCROLL. INSTEAD OF
CUTTING STRAIGHT DOWN HERE, REMOVE THE WOOD AT
AN ANGLE (FIG. 5). IF YOU GO PAST THE 1/4" WIDE
CUT, THAT'S O.K. BECAUSE THE NEXT STEP WILL BE TO
ROUND OVER THE WOOD THAT COMPRISES THE ROPE.

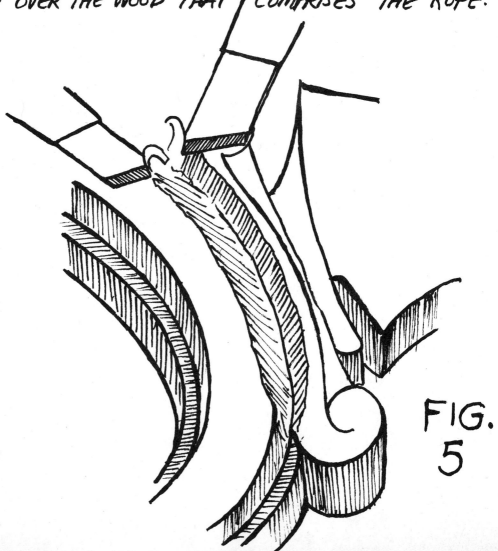

FIG.
5

STEP 6 · ROUNDING THE ROPE

USING THE PUSH METHOD, CARVE AWAY THE RAISED CORNERS EQUALLY ON BOTH SIDES, LEAVING ABOUT 1/4" OF FLAT AREA ON TOP (FIG. 6). THEN YOU CAN ROUND OVER THE ROPE (SEE END VIEW). YOU SHOULD HAVE NO FLAT AREAS ON THE ROPE & YOUR ROUNDING SHOULD GO ALL THE WAY TO THE ROPE'S EDGE. BUT BE CAREFUL AT THE VERY TOP THAT YOU DON'T TAKE MUCH IF ANY WOOD OFF BECAUSE YOU WILL END UP CHANGING THE THICKNESS OF THE ROPE.

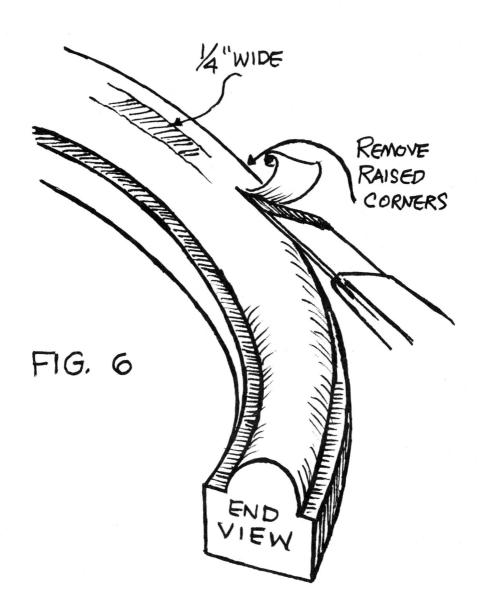

1/4" WIDE

REMOVE RAISED CORNERS

FIG. 6

END VIEW

STEP 7 · A PATTERN FOR THE ROPING

CUT OUT TWO PIECES OF WOOD ACCORDING TO THE FULL SIZE PATTERN IN FIG. 7. GLUE & NAIL THEM TOGETHER AT THE PRECISE ANGLE SHOWN. NOTICE THAT THE 1/4" THICK PIECE HAS A SLIGHT TAPER TO IT. DUPLICATE THIS EXACTLY.

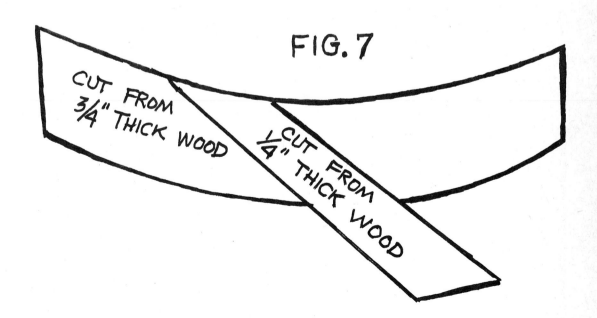

FIG. 7

CUT FROM 3/4" THICK WOOD

CUT FROM 1/4" THICK WOOD

STEP 8 · DRAWING THE ROPE STRANDS

HOLD THE PATTERN MADE IN THE PREVIOUS STEP
SNUGLY AGAINST THE INSIDE PERIMETER OF THE
MIRROR & DRAW LINES FOR THE ROPE (FIG. 8).
BECAUSE THE ROPE IS ROUNDED, YOU WILL HAVE
TO HOLD YOUR PENCIL PERFECTLY STRAIGHT UP
AND DOWN TO GET THESE LINES. CONTINUE TO
GO AROUND THE FRAME, DRAWING THESE LINES
THE WIDTH OF THE PATTERN. HOPEFULLY, THESE
LINES WILL COME OUT EVENLY WHEN YOU MEET
FROM WHERE YOU BEGAN. IF THEY DON'T,
ERASE THE LAST 3 OR 4 LINES & MAKE EACH
A LITTLE LARGER OR SMALLER SO THERE ISN'T
AN ODD ONE.

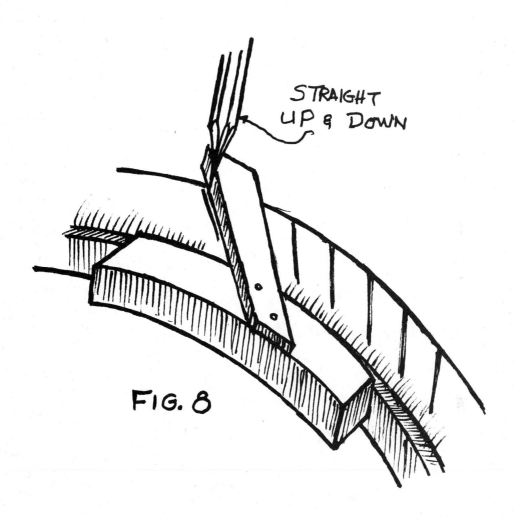

STRAIGHT
UP & DOWN

FIG. 8

STEP 9. DEFINING THE ROPE STRANDS

AGAIN WITH THE MCCARTHY KNIFE, CUT STRAIGHT DOWN ON EACH OF THE ROPE LINES (FIG. 9A). IN MAKING THIS STOP CUT, USE A ROCKING MOTION TO PREVENT ANY SPLITTING OR CHIPPING OF EACH SEGMENT. AFTER ALL YOUR STOP CUTS ARE MADE, CUT EACH SIDE AT AN ANGLE TO REMOVE WOOD (FIG. 9B). USE THE ILLUSTRATION AS A GUIDE FOR THE AMOUNT OF WOOD REMOVED. THESE CUTS DO NOT GO ALL THE WAY TO THE ROPE'S BASE, BUT ONLY ABOUT HALFWAY DOWN.

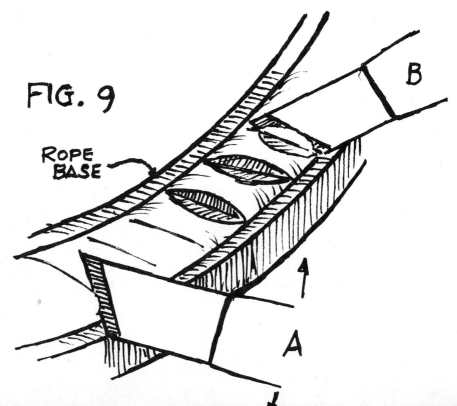

FIG. 9

ROPE BASE

B

A

STEP 10 · SHAPING THE ROPE STRANDS

FOLLOWING THE PRECISE ANGLE OF THE PREVIOUSLY MADE CUTS, CONTINUE TO CARVE DOWN TO THE ROPE'S BASE USING THE POINT OF THE KNIFE (FIG.10). IN THIS STEP, IT IS VERY EASY TO GET THE INDIVIDUAL STRANDS OUT OF ALIGNMENT. BE SURE TO FOLLOW EACH LINE'S DIRECTION INTO THE ROPE'S BASE.

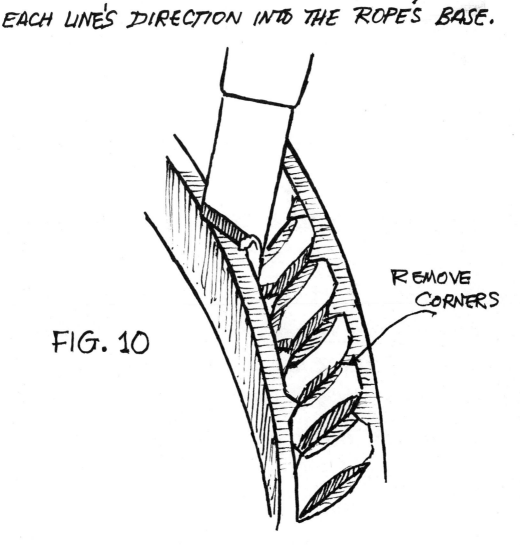

REMOVE CORNERS

FIG. 10

STEP 11· ROUNDING THE STRANDS

USING A #5 FISHTAIL GOUGE (SEE UNDER TOOLS NEEDED FOR SIZE), CARVE EACH STRAND WITH THE TOOL HELD UPSIDE DOWN (FIG. 11A). THE SHAPE OF THIS TOOL WILL ALLOW YOU TO ACHIEVE EXCELLENT ROUNDING. NEXT, ROUND EACH STRAND OVER INTO THE ROPE'S BASE (FIG. 11B), MAKING DEFINITE STOP CUTS. YOUR FINISHED STRANDS SHOULD HAVE THE ILLUSION OF ROUNDING & DISAPPEARING INTO THE BASE (FIG. 12).

AFTER THE ROPE HAS BEEN ROUNDED, SANDPAPER ALL ROPE STRANDS. THE ROPE'S BASE HAS PROBABLY BEEN MARKED & CUT INTO DURING THE PREVIOUS CARVING. THE LAST STEP IS TO RE-CARVE THE ROPE BASE TO FLATTEN IT EQUALLY ON BOTH SIDES & TO REMOVE ANY KNIFE CUTS OR MARKS (FIG. 13). IN THE AREA DIRECTLY BELOW THE SCROLL AND SHIP, YOU MAY NOT BE ABLE TO CONTINUE YOUR ROPE UNTIL YOU HAVE DONE SOME CARVING ON THESE SHAPES.

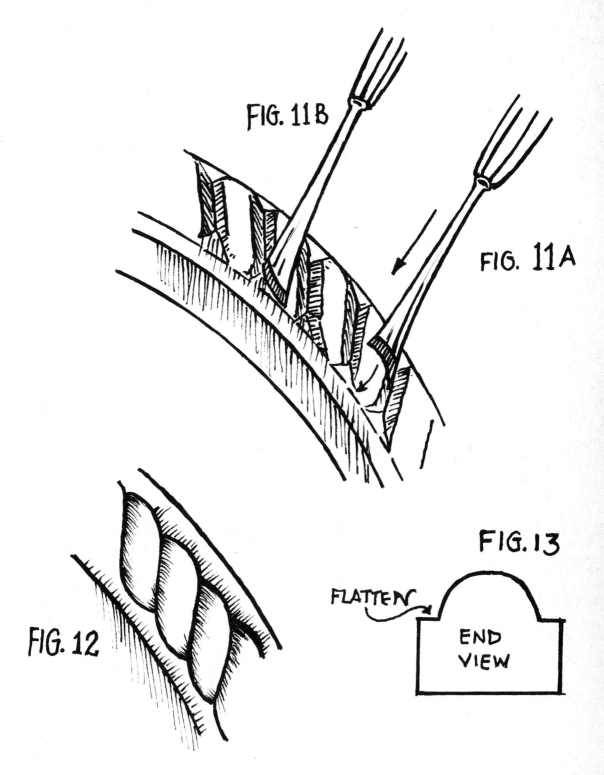

FIG. 11 B

FIG. 11 A

FIG. 12

FIG. 13

FLATTEN

END VIEW

STEP 12 · SHAPING THE SHIP

BECAUSE YOU ARE WORKING WITH THREE DEFINITE DEPTH LEVELS IN CARVING THIS SHIP ORNAMENTATION, IT WILL BE NECESSARY TO REMOVE A VOLUME OF WOOD FROM THE SAILS' SURFACE (FIG. 14). YOU CAN CARVE THIS AREA AWAY WITH A FISHTAIL GOUGE (FIG. 15). CARVE AS EVENLY & AS FLATLY AS POSSIBLE. DON'T BE WORRIED WHEN YOU CARVE AWAY THE SAIL LINES. THESE YOU'LL HAVE TO TRANSFER BACK FROM THE PATTERN WITH CARBON PAPER.

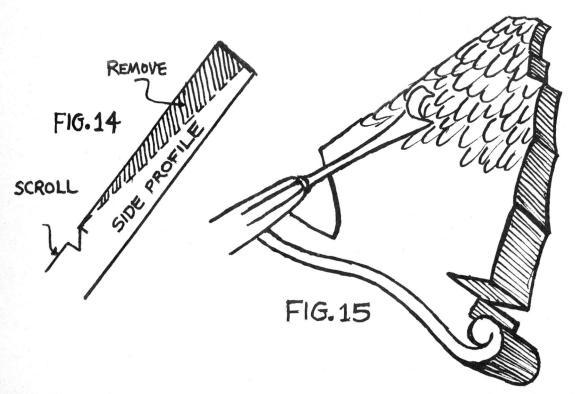

REMOVE

FIG. 14

SCROLL

SIDE PROFILE

FIG. 15

STEP 13 · SHAPING THE JIB SAILS

DRAW LINES ON THE SHIP TO APPROXIMATE THE DOTTED LINES IN FIG. 16. LEAVE A ¼" SPACE AS ILLUSTRATED AT THE EDGE. AGAIN WITH THE FISHTAIL, REMOVE WOOD FROM THIS AREA TO FORM A CONVEX ARC (FIG. 17). DO THIS EVENLY UP THE ENTIRE LENGTH OF THE SAILS. WITH THE McCARTHY KNIFE, FLATTEN (REMOVE ALL GOUGE MARKS) & SAND SMOOTH.

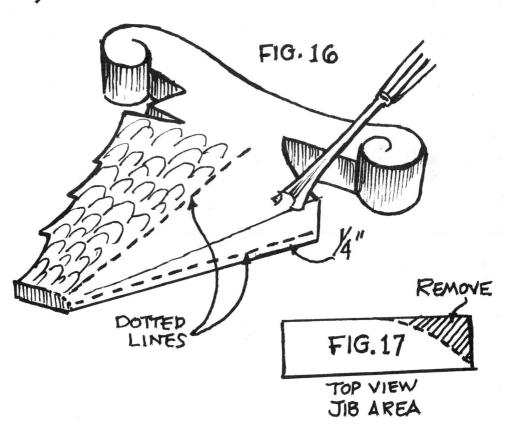

FIG. 16

DOTTED LINES

¼"

FIG. 17

REMOVE

TOP VIEW JIB AREA

STEP 14· CARVING THE SAILS

IF YOU HAVEN'T DONE SO ALREADY, TRANSFER THE SAIL PATTERN ONTO WOOD. USING THE McCARTHY KNIFE, CARVE STRAIGHT DOWN ONTO THE BACK EDGES OF EACH GROUP OF SAILS (FIG.18) & REMOVE A 3/8" WIDE BY 1/4" DEEP PIECE OF WOOD. MAKE EACH CUT SO IT FORMS A HALF 'V' (FIG.19). MAKE THIS CUT ALONG GROUPS 1, 2, & 3 AND BOTH JIB SAILS. ALL THE LINES GOING ACROSS THE SAILS & THE YARDARMS ARE DONE WITH A 'V' CUT.

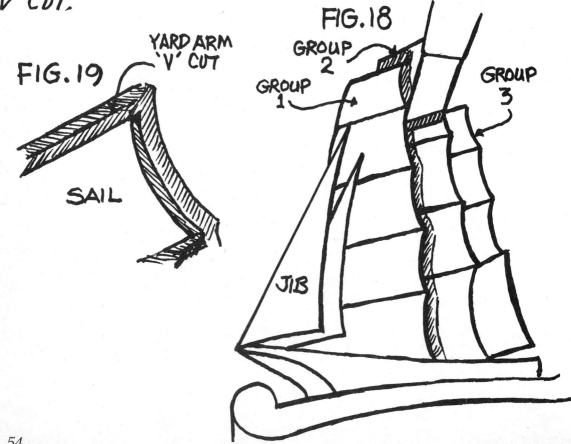

FIG.18

YARDARM 'V' CUT

FIG.19

GROUP 2

GROUP 1

GROUP 3

SAIL

JIB

STEP 15 · CARVING THE SAILS (CONTINUED)

YOU WILL HAVE TO CARVE THE SAILS TO GIVE THEM THE ILLUSION OF BEING STEPPED BACK. TO DO THIS, LAY THE KNIFE FLAT & WORK FROM THE REAR EDGES OF THE SAILS (FIG. 20). REMOVE ¼" OF WOOD AT THE EDGE OF EACH PRECEDING SAIL. ALSO, DON'T START AT THE VERY EDGE OF A SAIL, BUT LEAVE ¼" OF FLAT AREA. FIGURE 21 SHOWS THE FINAL ANGLES OF THE SAILS. MAKE SURE THE ANGLES FOR EACH GROUPING ARE EQUAL IN DEPTH.

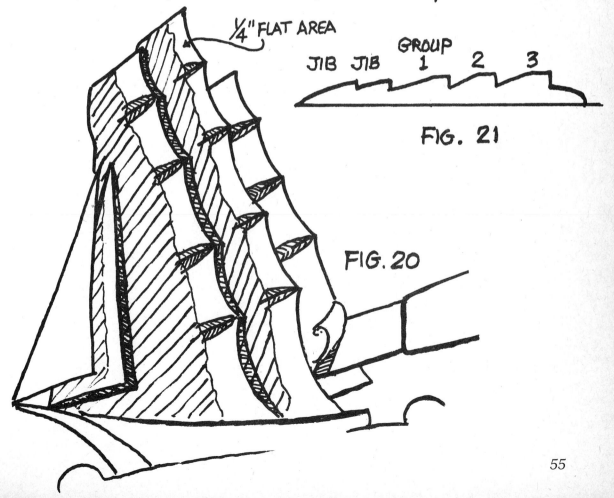

¼" FLAT AREA

GROUP
JIB JIB   1   2   3

FIG. 21

FIG. 20

STEP 16 · BILLOWING THE SAILS

BY LAYING THE KNIFE FLAT, ROUND OVER EACH SAIL FROM ITS TOP TO ITS BOTTOM SO NO FLAT SURFACES REMAIN. SEE THE END VIEW IN FIG. 22. FOR THE YARD-ARM GROOVES, EASE IN THE POINT OF THE BLADE AS TIGHTLY AS YOU CAN AND SNIP OUT THE WOOD (FIG. 23A). CONCENTRATE TO MAINTAIN ALL YARDARMS STRAIGHT AND PARALLEL WITH ALL OTHERS. THE ONLY EXCEPTION IS THE REAR SAIL WHICH IS CUT LATER AT A DIF-FERENT ANGLE (FIG. 23B).

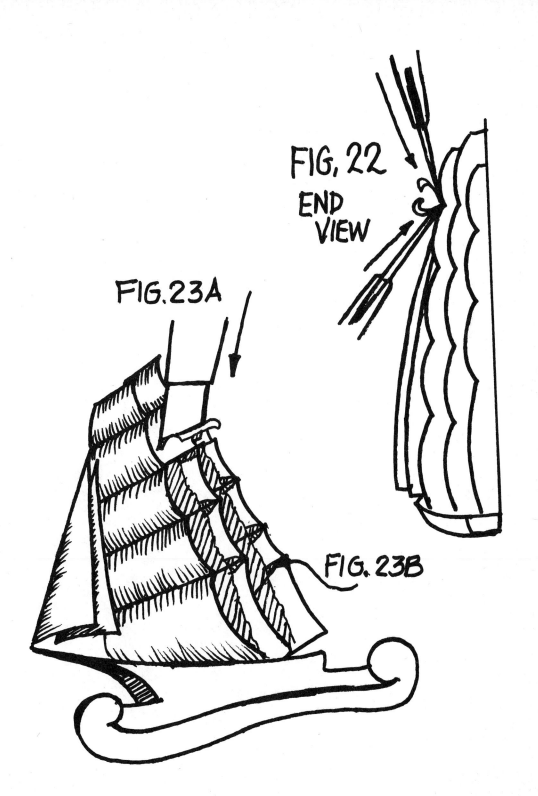

FIG. 22
END
VIEW

FIG. 23A

FIG. 23B

STEP 17 • FINISHING THE BILLOWS

USING THE SAIL PATTERN, SKETCH IN THE ARCS AT THE LOWER EDGES OF THE SAILS, INCLUDING THE JIBS. CUT STRAIGHT DOWN & AT AN ANGLE ALONG THESE LINES (FIGS. 24A+B & 25A+B). REMOVE WOOD A LITTLE AT A TIME FROM THE TOPS OF THE SAILS (FIG. 25 C), SMOOTHING SURFACES INTO SLIGHT ARC (FIGS. 24 & 25 B+C).

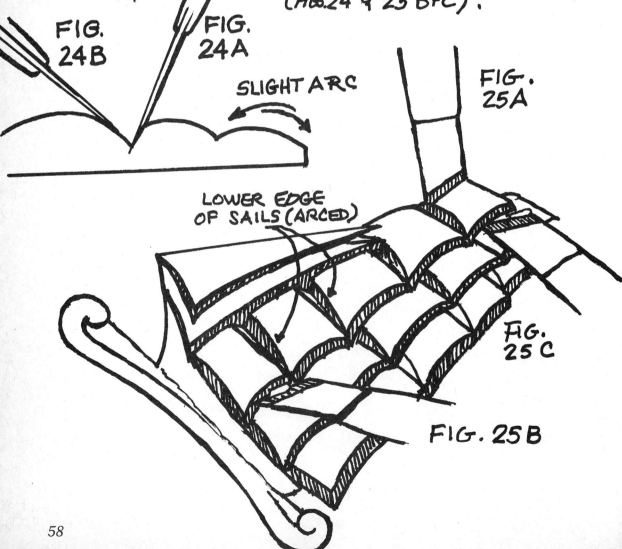

FIG. 24B

FIG. 24A

SLIGHT ARC

FIG. 25A

LOWER EDGE OF SAILS (ARCED)

FIG. 25 C

FIG. 25 B

STEP 18 · FINAL CLEANUP OF JIBS AND MAKING THE HULL

PRIOR TO SANDING, YOU WILL HAVE TO GO BACK OVER EACH JIB SAIL & FINISH SHAPING THEM AS CLEANLY AS YOU CAN. BY LAYING YOUR KNIFE FLAT, CARVE UP THE FIRST JIB (FIG. 26A), SMOOTHING BUT MAINTAINING A GRADUAL ARC (FIG. 26B). BRING THE KNIFE ALONG THE FRONT OF THE JIB TO GIVE IT A SHARP EDGE (FIG. 26C) & TO CARVE AWAY SAW MARKS. YOU CAN CARVE THE EDGE BACK AT A SLIGHT ANGLE TO CREATE A SHADOW WHEN THE MIRROR IS FINALLY HUNG ON THE WALL. ALSO CARVE BACK BEHIND THE FIRST JIB AT A SLIGHT ANGLE (FIG. 26D) BEFORE SMOOTHING THE SECOND. REMEMBER THAT BOTH JIBS ARE THE SAME SHAPE, BUT THE SECOND IS STEPPED BACK FROM THE FIRST. DURING ALL THIS SAIL CARVING, YOU SHOULD HAVE DROPPED THE SAILS QUITE A BIT BACK FROM THE HULL.

STEP 18 · CONTINUED ⟶

STEP 18· CONTINUED

REFFERING TO FIG. 27, SKETCH IN THE TOP OF THE
HULL LINE & CARVE AWAY THE EXCESS INTO WHAT
WILL BECOME THE WATER. NOTE THAT THE SIDES
OF A SHIP ARE NOT STRAIGHT UP AND DOWN, THEY
ARE WIDER AT THE TOP OF THE HULL THAN AT THE
WATERLINE.

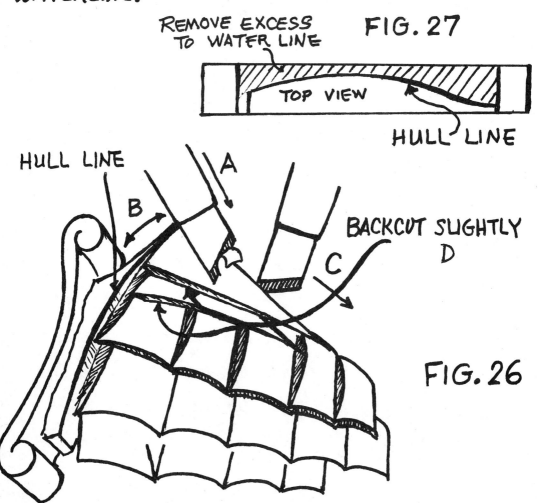

REMOVE EXCESS
TO WATER LINE

FIG. 27

TOP VIEW

HULL LINE

HULL LINE

A

B

BACKCUT SLIGHTLY
D

C

FIG. 26

STEP 19 · CLEANING UP REMAINING SAILS

YOU WANT EACH SAIL TO ARC OR BOW FROM TOP TO BOTTOM, NOT SIDE TO SIDE. TO DO THIS, FIND THE CENTERLINE OF EACH SAIL (FIG. 28A). THEN LAY YOUR KNIFE ALMOST FLAT TO THE SAIL & PUSH FROM THE REAR EDGE FORWARD TO FORM A GRADUAL ARC (FIG. 28 B). AS YOU MOVE BACK FROM ONE SET OF SAILS TO ANOTHER, BE SURE TO MAINTAIN THE ARCS OF THE REAR EDGES (FIG. 28 C).

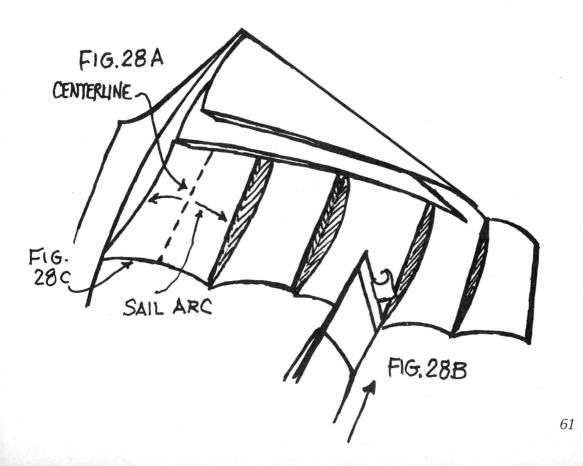

FIG. 28 A

CENTERLINE

FIG. 28 C

SAIL ARC

FIG. 28 B

STEP 20 · MAKING THE YARDARMS

AT THE TOP OF EACH SQUARE SAIL (NOT THE JIBS), SKETCH IN PARALLEL LINES TO ESTABLISH THE YARDARMS. MAKE THESE ABOUT 1/8" WIDE. NEXT, REMOVE A 1/8" WIDE BY 1/8" DEEP 'V' FROM DIRECTLY BENEATH EACH YARDARM (FIGS. 29A & B). AFTER YOU HAVE EX-POSED THE YARDARMS, LAY YOUR BLADE FLAT AND RESHAPE THE SAILS' SURFACES INTO THE YARDARMS WITH GRADUAL ARCS (FIGS. 29C & 30). ROUND OVER EACH YARDARM SLIGHTLY BEFORE SANDING. MAKE SURE THEY ARE UNIFORM IN SIZE & PARALLEL. TRY TO TAPER THE ENDS A LITTLE.

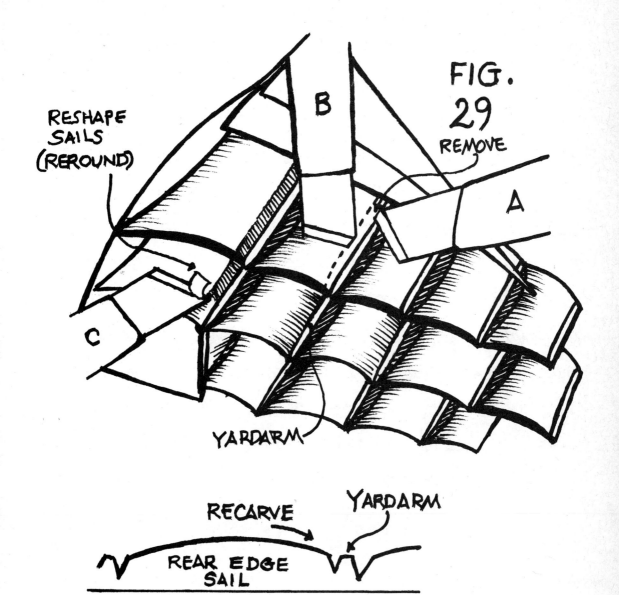

RESHAPE SAILS (REROUND)

FIG. 29

REMOVE

B

A

C

YARDARM

RECARVE

YARDARM

REAR EDGE SAIL

FIG. 30

STEP 21 · FINAL TOUCHES ON THE SAILS

WHERE THE JIB MEETS THE HULL, THERE SHOULD BE A SEPARATION. CLEAN UP THE BOTTOM ARC OF THE JIBS AND CARVE ALONG THE SHEAR OF THE HULL (SHEAR IS THE SWEEP OF THE HULL LINE). NOTICE THE SLIGHT ARC AT THE TOP OF THE HULL (FIG. 31A). BUT AS IT REACHES THE BOWSPRIT IT STRAIGHTENS (FIG. 31B), THIS IS BECAUSE THE BOWSPRIT IS FAIRLY STRAIGHT. CARVE THE BOWSPRIT SO IT IS NARROW & TAPERS MORE TO A POINT TOWARD ITS END. THE AREAS BETWEEN THE TOP OF THE BOWSPRIT AND THE BOTTOM OF THE JIBS IS CARVED INTO A DEEP 'V' TO ACCENT THEM. CARVE A SMALL 'V' AT THE BOTTOM OF THE SECOND JIB (FIG. 31C) TO ACCENT ITS ARC.

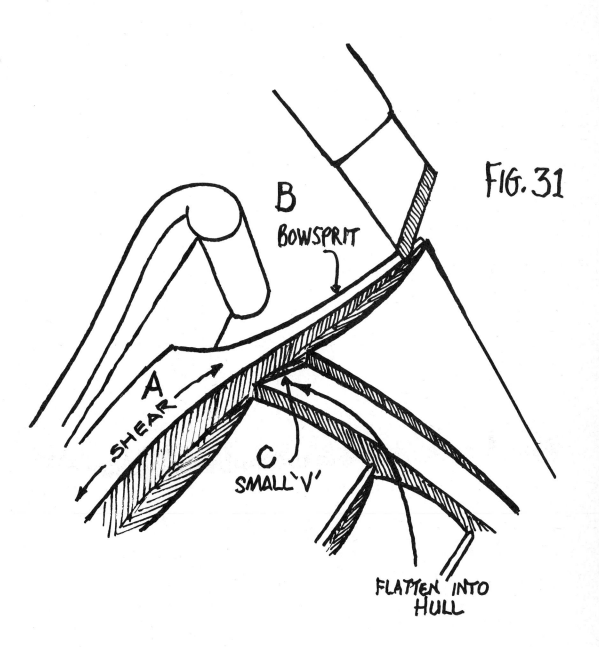

B
BOWSPRIT

FIG. 31

A
SHEAR

C
SMALL 'V'

FLATTEN INTO
HULL

STEP 22. THE SPANKER SAIL

THERE IS STILL ONE MORE SAIL YOU WILL HAVE TO DEAL WITH AND THAT IS THE SPANKER SAIL WHICH IS THE LAST SAIL AT THE END OF THE SHIP (FIG. 32 & 33A). IT IS NOT A SQUARE RIGGED SAIL BUT A GAFF-RIGGED ONE. WHILE THE YARDARMS ARE AT RIGHT ANGLES TO THE MASTS, THE GAFF ANGLES UPWARD FROM THE MAST. CARVE THE GAFF & THE BOOM (FIG. 33B&C) AS YOU DID THE YARDARMS. AFTER ALL THE SAILS & YARDARMS HAVE BEEN COMPLETELY SHAPED, SMOOTH EACH WITH 120 GRIT SANDPAPER.

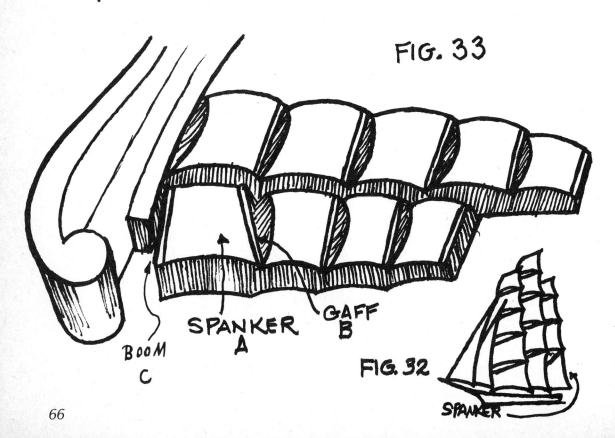

FIG. 33

SPANKER
A

GAFF
B

BOOM
C

FIG. 32

SPANKER

STEP 23 · SHAPING THE SCROLLWORK AND WATER
USING THE KNIFE HELD FLAT, CARVE AWAY THE SURFACE
OF THE SCROLLWORK SO IT CONFORMS TO THE SHAPE OF
THE HULL. CARVE FROM THE CENTER OF THE SCROLL
TOWARD THE BOW & THEN TOWARD THE STERN (FIG. 34).
GIVE THIS AREA A SLIGHT ARC WITH BOTH ENDS LOWER
THAN THE MIDSHIP (FIG. 35).

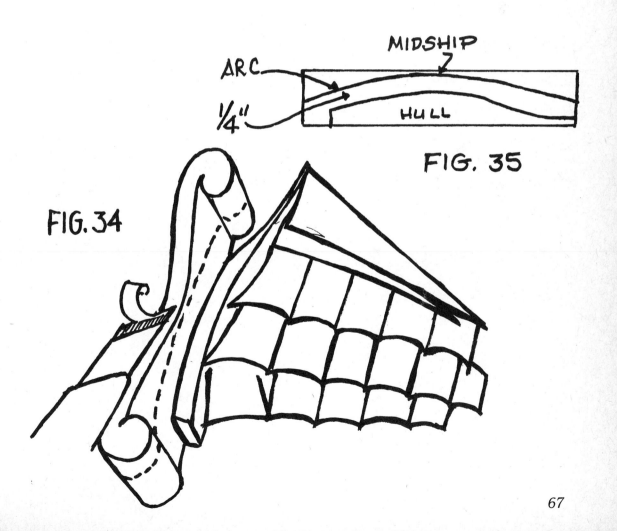

ARC

MIDSHIP

1/4"

HULL

FIG. 35

FIG. 34

STEP 24 · CARVING THE SCROLL

SKETCH IN THE SCROLL & CUT STRAIGHT DOWN WITH THE KNIFE TO SEPARATE IT FROM THE WATER (FIG. 36). MAKE THE SCROLLWORK ABOUT 1/4" WIDE & CUT A HALF 'V' FROM THE WATER INTO THE SCROLL 1/8" DEEP. YOU WANT TO CUT INTO THE WATER SO THE SCROLL HAS A HALF ROUNDED APPEARANCE. WITH THE FISHTAIL GOUGE USED PREVIOUSLY FOR THE ROPE STRANDS, CUT STRAIGHT DOWN AROUND THE BALLS AT THE ENDS & REMOVE WOOD AT AN ANGLE (FIG. 37). ROUND BALLS COMPLETELY INTO THE GOUGE CUTS. LEAVE A SHARP EDGE AS NOTED IN FIG. 37. WHEN FINISHED WITH THE CONCAVE CARVING, YOU CAN TURN THE GOUGE OVER & ROUND THE REMAINING SCROLLWORK (FIG. 38).

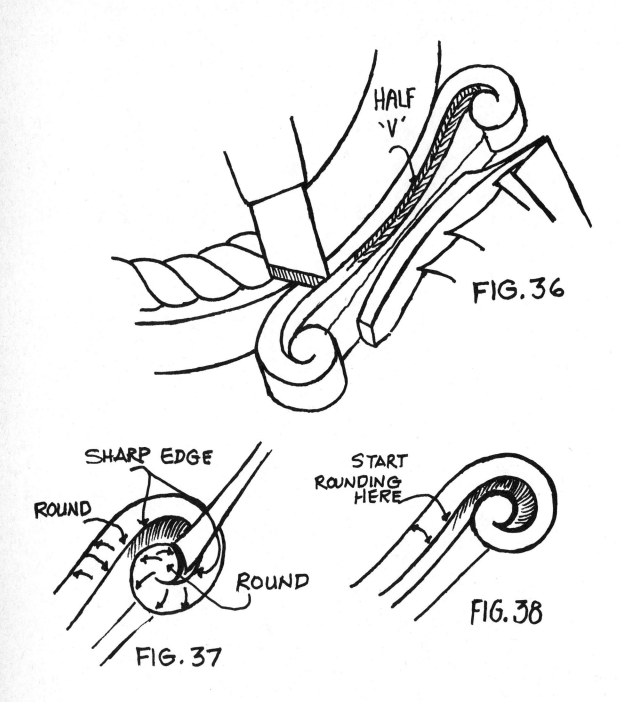

HALF 'V'

FIG. 36

SHARP EDGE

ROUND

ROUND

FIG. 37

START ROUNDING HERE

FIG. 38

STEP 25• MAKING THE WATER

You SHOULD HAVE A RIDGE REMAINING AT THE TOP OF
THE WATER THAT FOLLOWS THE CONTOUR OF THE HULL
(FIG. 39A). FOLLOWING THE HULL, CARVE THIS AWAY
WITH THE KNIFE AT A 45° ANGLE (FIG. 39B). THIS WILL
BRING THE RIDGE LOWER THAN THE SCROLL (FIG 39C).
TRY TO FLATTEN THE WATER AS MUCH AS YOU CAN AS
YOU REACH THE HULL.

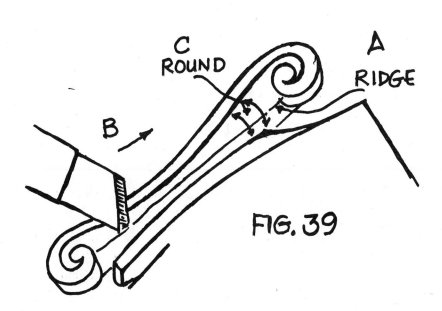

FIG. 39

STEP 26 · MAKING WAVES

WHERE THE HULL & THE TOP OF THE WATER MEET, CUT STRAIGHT DOWN WITH THE KNIFE, BUT AS YOU CUT FROM BOW TO STERN, MAKE THE LINE WAVY (FIG 40A). NOW WITH A V PARTING TOOL, CARVE INTO THE WATER AREA WITH SHORT, 1" to 1½" LONG STROKES WITH A WAVY MOTION (40B). BUT KEEP THE CUTS PARALLEL TO THE HULL LINE. MAKE THESE CUTS AS CLOSE AS YOU CAN, LEAVING AS FEW FLAT AREAS AS POSSIBLE. STAGGER & OVERLAP THEM. BE CAREFUL NOT TO FOLLOW THE ARC OF THE SCROLLWORK. IT MIGHT HELP TO SKETCH IN LINES. SAND THE HULL & SCROLLWORK SURFACES.

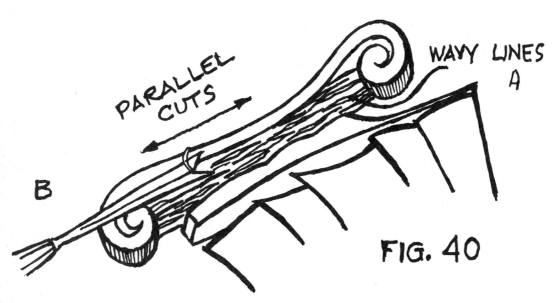

PARALLEL CUTS

WAVY LINES
A

B

FIG. 40

STEP 27 · BACKCUTTING

UP TO THIS POINT, ALL THE SHIP CARVING HAS BEEN DONE ON THE FRONT. NOW YOU WILL HAVE TO TURN OVER THE MIRROR & REMOVE WOOD FROM THE BACK TO GIVE THE SAILS THE ILLUSION OF BEING THIN.

SKETCH IN A PENCIL LINE ALONG THE EDGES OF THE REAR SAILS, LEAVING A 1/8" THICK EDGE (FIG. 41). WITH THE FISHTAIL, CARVE AWAY THE EXCESS WOOD AT AN ANGLE TOWARD THE BACK OF THE SHIP (FIG. 42). THE THINNER YOU CAN GET THOSE BACK EDGES OF THE SAILS, THE MORE GRACEFUL THE SHIP WILL APPEAR. ALSO, ROUND OVER THE SCROLL ENDS ON THEIR BACKS.

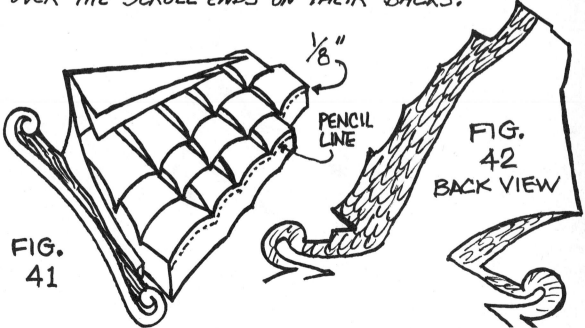

1/8"

PENCIL
LINE

FIG.
41

FIG.
42
BACK VIEW

STEP 28 · LOWERING THE EDGES

SKETCH IN A PENCIL LINE AROUND THE CIRCUMFERENCE OF BOTH THE INSIDE & OUTSIDE EDGES OF THE FRAME $\frac{7}{8}"$ FROM THE BOTTOM (FIG. 43 & 44A). WITH THE POINT OF THE KNIFE, CARVE THE EDGE AT AN ANGLE FROM THE ROPING TO THE PENCIL LINE (FIG. 44B). BE SURE YOU GO WITH THE GRAIN TO AVOID SPLINTERING. DO THIS FOR BOTH THE INSIDE & THE OUTSIDE EDGES.

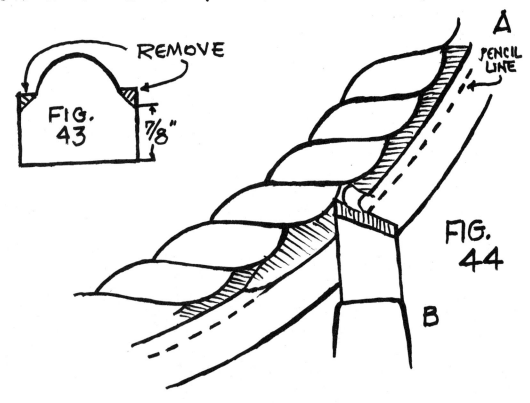

REMOVE

FIG. 43

$\frac{7}{8}"$

A

PENCIL LINE

FIG. 44

B

STEP 29 · FINISHING THE FRAME EDGES

USING THE FISHTAIL GOUGE, CARVE AWAY THE SAW MARKS FROM FRAME EDGES, LEAVING A CHIP-CARVED PATTERN (FIG. 45). TO KEEP YOURSELF CARVING IN THE RIGHT DIRECTION, FOLLOW THE GRAIN PATTERN (ARROWS) IN FIG. 46.

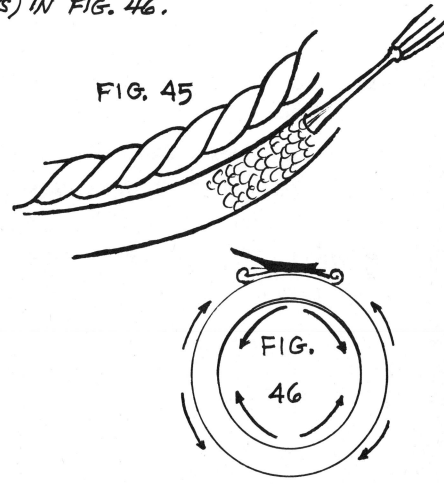

FIG. 45

FIG. 46

STEP 30 · SLOTTING FOR THE MIRROR

TURN THE FRAME OVER AGAIN & SKETCH IN PENCIL LINES 3/8" WIDE FROM THE INSIDE EDGE AND 3/8" DOWN FROM THE TOP (FIG. 47). THIS IS WOOD TO BE REMOVED, AND A MACHINE LIKE A ROUTER WILL TAKE AWAY THE WOOD FASTER, BUT HANDCARVING WILL TEACH YOU MORE. REMOVE WOOD AT AN ANGLE WITH THE KNIFE (FIG. 48), FOLLOWING THE GRAIN PATTERN IN FIG. 46. WHEN A BULK OF THE WOOD HAS BEEN REMOVED, CUT STRAIGHT DOWN AND STRAIGHT IN TO FORM THE RIGHT-ANGLED SLOT. MAKE SURE THE SLOT FOR THE MIRROR IS FLAT & EVEN. THIS SHOULD ACCOMMODATE A 13¾" DIAMETER MIRROR, BUT CHECK THE DIMENSION BEFORE PURCHASING IT.

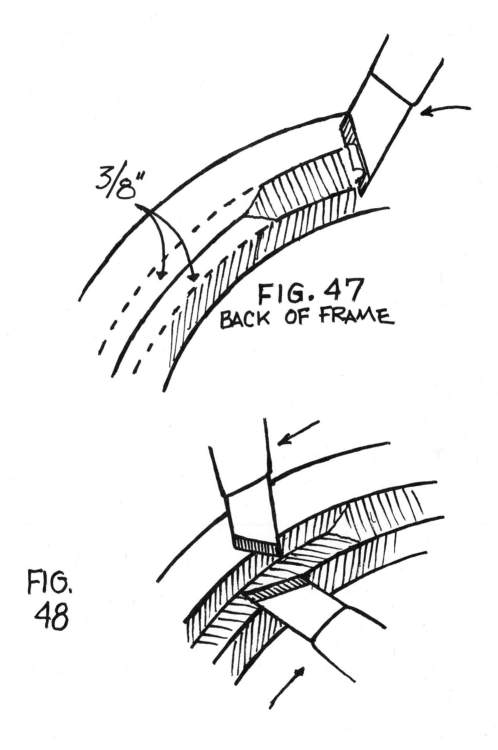

3/8"

FIG. 47
BACK OF FRAME

FIG.
48

STEP 31 · COLORING THE FRAME

BEFORE INSERTING THE MIRROR, YOU WILL WANT TO FINISH THE FRAME. A GOOD CHOICE OF STAIN MIGHT BE JACOBEAN (MINWAX). PUT THIS ON THE ENTIRE FRAME. AFTER IT HAS DRIED (ALLOW AT LEAST A DAY), USE A SATIN FINISH POLYURETHANE TO COMPLETELY SEAL THE WOOD. GIVE AT LEAST 4 COATS, SANDING LIGHTLY BETWEEN APPLICATIONS WITH 400 GRIT WET-DRY SANDPAPER.

USE A SLOW SET GOLD LEAF SIZE AND APPLY IT TO THE ROPING & SCROLLWORK. AFTER WAITING FOR THE SIZE TO GET TACKY, PROBABLY 16 - 24 HOURS, APPLY THE GOLD LEAF. WITH PAINT YOU CAN MAKE THE SAILS WHITE, BUT YOU MIGHT PREFER TO LET THE WOOD YOU WORKED SO HARD ON TO SHOW THROUGH BY USING STAINS.

STEP 32. A MIRROR TO LOOK INTO

YOU CAN OBTAIN A MIRROR AT MOST GLASS SUPPLY STORES, PURCHASE ONE 1/4" THICK. YOU SHOULD BACK THIS UP WITH A 1/8" THICK PIECE OF HARDBOARD OR PLYWOOD. THIS AND THE MIRROR CAN BE HELD WITH GLAZIER'S PUSH POINTS OR SMALL WIRE BRADS. A HANGER SHOULD BE PUT INTO THE FRAME BENEATH THE SHIP, OR YOU CAN USE A WIRE WITH TWO SCREW EYES.

The Rose
a wall hanging

TOOLS
NEEDED

McCARTHY KNIFE

FISHTAIL GOUGE

JACKKNIFE

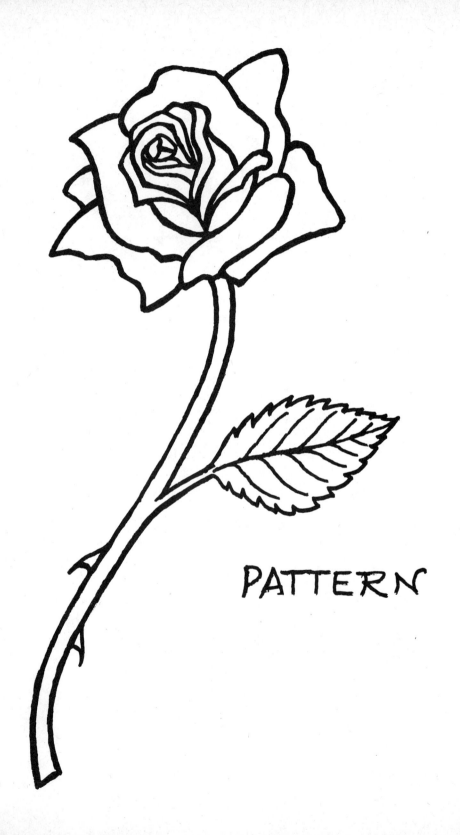

PATTERN

STEP 1 · SELECTING THE WOOD

THE WOOD FOR THIS PLAQUE SHOULD NOT BE GLUED UP BUT SOLID. YOU WILL HAVE TO FIND A PIECE AT LEAST 1" THICK & ABOUT 10" WIDE, 14" LONG (A 1"x10" IN A LUMBERYARD MEASURES ONLY 3/4" x 9¼", SO YOU WOULD HAVE TO GO WITH A 5/4"x12" WHICH SHOULD MEASURE 1⅛" x 11¼".) EASTERN WHITE PINE, KNOT-FREE, WAS USED FOR THIS PROJECT. IT HAS NICE GRAIN THAT IS FAIRLY EASY TO CARVE, AND IT TAKES STAINS AND PAINT WELL. OTHER WOOD SUCH AS BASSWOOD, MAHOGANY, & BLACK WALNUT, ALL HARDWOODS, COULD BE USED. AFTER FINDING YOUR WOOD, TRANSFER THE PATTERN ONTO IT, MAKING SURE IT IS CENTERED. DRAW LINES 1" IN FROM THE EDGES OF THE BOARD FOR THE BORDER (FIG. 1).

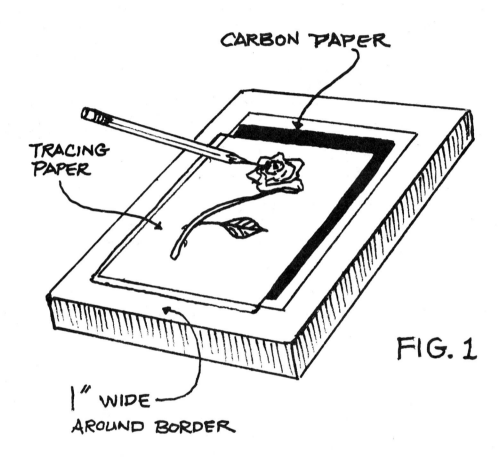

CARBON PAPER

TRACING PAPER

1" WIDE AROUND BORDER

FIG. 1

STEP 2 · SEPARATING THE ROSE AND BORDER

USING THE McCARTHY KNIFE, CUT STRAIGHT DOWN ALONG THE INNER EDGE OF THE BORDER (FIG. 2) AND ALSO AROUND THE ROSE. THIS IS THE STOP CUT THAT WILL PREVENT CHIPPING AWAY ANY OF THE FLOWER OR BORDER. REMOVE WEDGES OF WOOD BY CUTTING AT AN ANGLE INTO THE STOP CUTS (FIG. 3 END VIEW). CARVE IT AWAY A LITTLE AT A TIME UNTIL YOU REACH A 3/8" DEPTH.

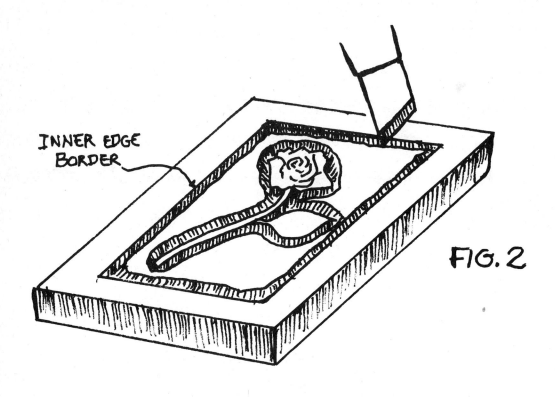

INNER EDGE
BORDER

FIG. 2

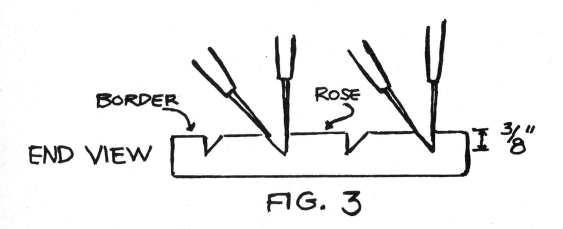

BORDER

ROSE

END VIEW

$\frac{3}{8}$"

FIG. 3

STEP 3. REMOVING THE BACKGROUND

USE A FISHTAIL GOUGE AND REMOVE THE BACK-GROUND EVENLY TO THE 3/8" DEPTH, LEAVING THE ROSE & BORDER UNTOUCHED (FIG. 4). BE CAREFUL AROUND THE ROSE NOT TO CHIP ANY OF IT AWAY. LEAVE GOUGE MARKS IN BACKGROUND FOR TEXTURE.

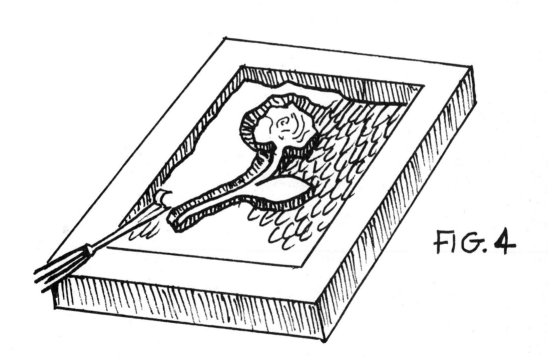

FIG. 4

STEP 4. LAYERING THE PETALS

IN CARVING THE FLOWER, YOU HAVE TO ESTABLISH DIFFERENT LEVELS FOR THE PETALS TO GIVE THE ROSE A THREE-DIMENSIONAL LOOK. THIS WILL HAVE TO BE DONE A LITTLE AT A TIME. START BY CUTTING STRAIGHT DOWN ALONG DARK LINES IN FIG. 5A AND REMOVE THE WOOD FROM THE PETAL SURFACES (FIG. 5B) AT AN ANGLE. LOWER THESE OUTSIDE PETALS 1, 2, 3, 4, & 5, AND THEN THE STEM, TO ABOUT ONE-HALF THE DEPTH OF THE FLOWER SURFACE. THEN GRADUALLY ROUND OVER THE PETALS SO THEIR OUTER EDGES ARE CLOSE TO THE BACKGROUND (FIG. 6 END VIEW). MAKE A CUT BETWEEN 1 AND 5 AND LOWER 5 SO IT LOOKS LIKE IT GOES BENEATH 1. DO THE SAME ON 3 AND 4, MAKING 3 LOWER THAN 4. THE LAYERING OF 2 IS NOT QUITE AS MUCH AS WITH 3. ALSO, DO NOT CARVE THESE INDIVIDUAL PETALS PERFECTLY FLAT. FOLLOW THE ARROW LINES FOR THE SHAPES OF THE PETALS (FIG. 5).

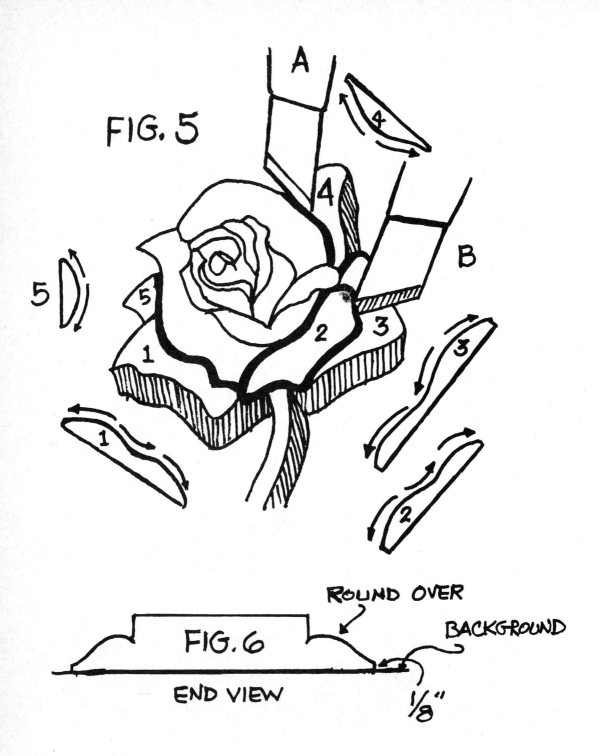

FIG. 5

A

B

ROUND OVER

BACKGROUND

FIG. 6

END VIEW

1/8"

STEP 5 · MORE LAYERING

FOLLOW THE SAME PROCEDURE FOR PETALS 6, 7, & 8, FOLLOWING THE BLACK LINES IN FIG. 7. ALSO CHECK THE CROSS-SECTIONAL OR PROFILE VIEWS (FIG. 7A, B & C). PETAL 8, HOWEVER, IS CARVED DIFFERENTLY FROM THE REST BECAUSE IT TWISTS AND ROLLS OVER ITSELF. THIS CAN BE DONE BY LOWERING THE LOWER HALF OF THE PETAL.

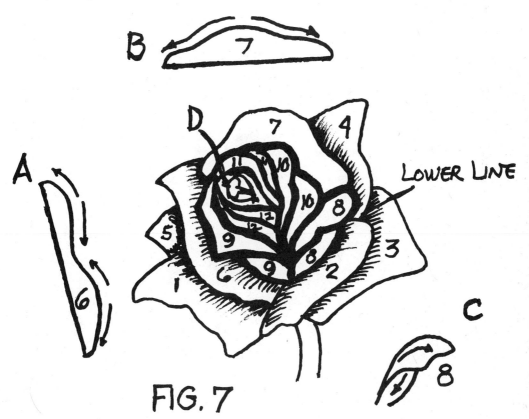

FIG. 7

STEP 6 · THE REMAINING PETALS

PETAL 9 IS ALSO ROLLED OVER SLIGHTLY. PETAL 10 HAS A CURLED LIP AND SHOULD GIVE THE APPEARANCE OF COVERING PETAL 7. IF IT IS DIFFICULT WORKING BETWEEN THESE PETALS AND CLOSE TO THE CENTER, YOU MAY WANT TO TRY A JACKKNIFE. PETAL 11 IS ALSO CURLED OR TWISTED SLIGHTLY. AND FINALLY, PETAL 12 COMES OUT AND THEN TURNS INTO THE CENTER SHARPLY. THE VERY CENTER CAN BE NOTCHED OUT WITH THE POINT OF YOUR JACKKNIFE, MAKING A DEEP 'V' (FIG. 70).

STEP 7. SHAPING THE STEM & LEAF

THE FLOWER STEM MUST STILL BE LOWERED SO IT APPEARS TO GO UNDER THE FLOWER. IT MUST ALSO BE ROUNDED SLIGHTLY. PLUS, THE STEM SHOULD GO UP AND DOWN AGAIN WHERE THE LEAF STEM IS (FIG. 8). THE UPPER EDGE OF THE LEAF SHOULD BE LOWER TO THE BACKGROUND, GIVING IT A TIPPED EFFECT. CARVE A SHALLOW 'V' DOWN THE CENTER OF THE LEAF AND FROM THIS CENTER ROUND OVER THE EDGES INTO THE BACKGROUND (FIG. 9). WITH THE POINT OF THE KNIFE, NOTCH THE EDGES OF THE LEAF INTO THE BACKGROUND (FIG. 10), THEN WITH SMALL 'V's CARVE THE LINES INTO THE LEAF,

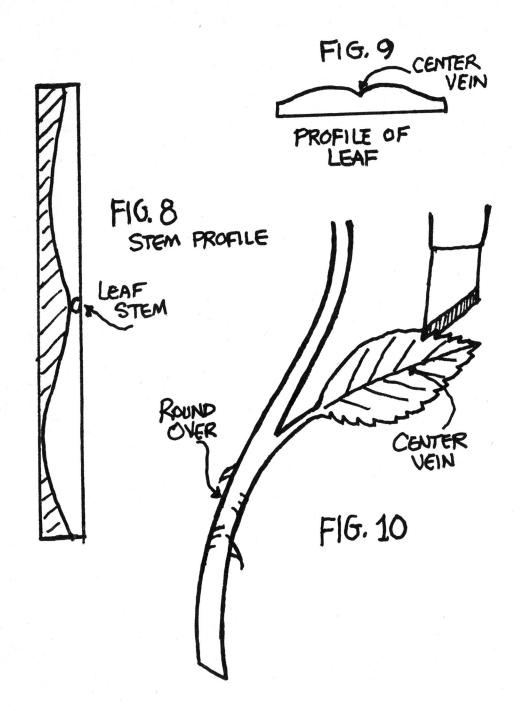

FIG. 9
CENTER VEIN
PROFILE OF LEAF

FIG. 8
STEM PROFILE

LEAF STEM

ROUND OVER

CENTER VEIN

FIG. 10

STEP 8 · FINISHING THE FRAME

WITH THE FISHTAIL GOUGE, DISTRESS THE FRAME, WORKING THE TOOL AROUND IT BUT IN THE SAME DIRECTION (FIG. 11).

CHIP CARVING IN SAME DIRECTION

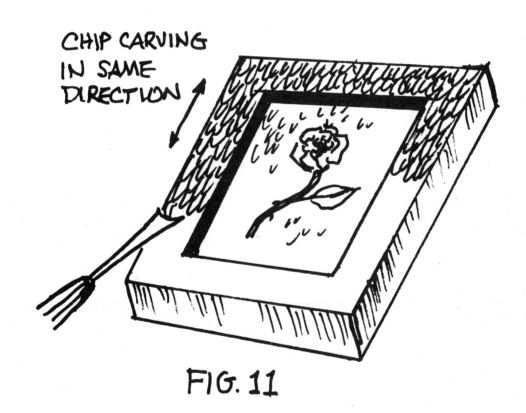

FIG. 11

STEP 9. FINISHING TOUCHES

THE BACKGROUND FOR THE ROSE PLAQUE CAN BE
COLORED WITH A GOLDEN OAK STAIN. THE REST
CAN BE DONE WITH UNIVERSAL TINTING COLORS.
YOU BEGIN WITH DIME SIZE SQUIRTS THAT ARE
DILUTED SLIGHTLY WITH TURPENTINE. JUST DUNK
YOUR BRUSH INTO THE TURPENTINE AND THEN INTO
YOUR TINTING COLOR & MIX TO A CONSISTENCY
OF STAIN (DO THIS ON A GLOSSY-PAGED MAG-
AZINE). FOR THE ROSE, USE EXTERIOR RED.
REMOVE ANY EXCESS WITH A RAG. THE STEM &
LEAF CAN BE DONE WITH THALO GREEN. YOU
CAN USE RAW UMBER TO ANTIQUE THE ROSE
BY STAINING DEEP INTO CREVICES & WIPING
WITH RAG. USE A LITTLE YELLOW ON ROSE
PETAL TIPS & LEAF TIPS SO COLORS ARE NOT
SO SOLID. FINISH THE FRAME & BACK WITH
WALNUT STAIN. SEAL UP THIS PROJECT WITH
3 COATS OF SATIN POLYURETHANE. IT IS NOW
READY TO BE HUNG.

Rainbow Trout

WALL PLAQUE

TOOLS NEEDED

JACKKNIFE

V PARTING TOOL

V

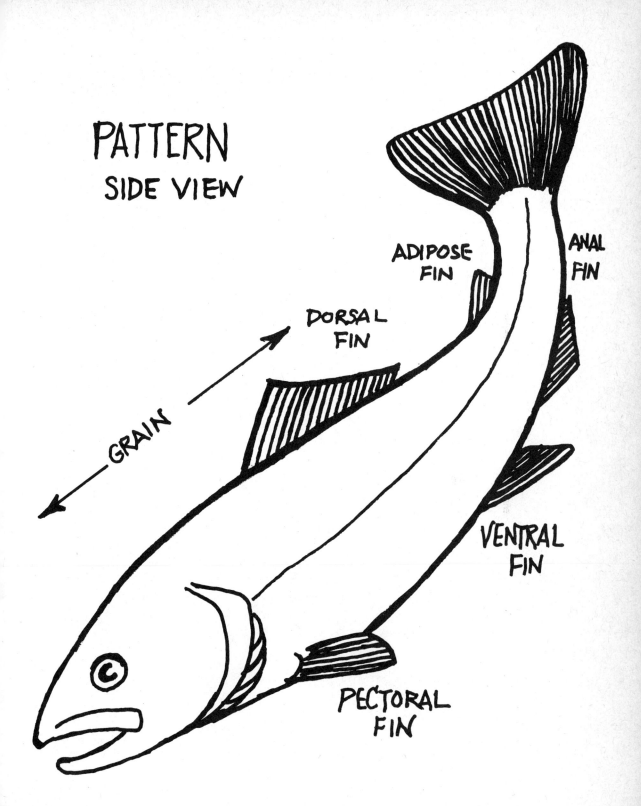

PATTERN
SIDE VIEW

GRAIN

DORSAL
FIN

ADIPOSE
FIN

ANAL
FIN

VENTRAL
FIN

PECTORAL
FIN

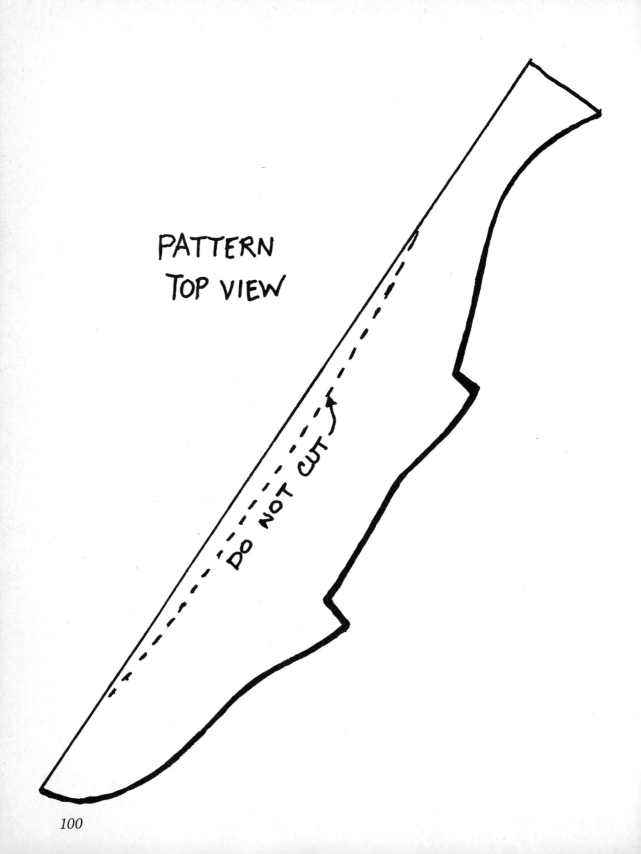

PATTERN
TOP VIEW

DO NOT CUT

STEP 1. USING A GRID

THIS CARVING IS A MINIATURE VERSION OF A RAIN-
BOW TROUT (THOUGH IN SOME INSTANCES IT MAY NOT
BE A MINIATURE AT ALL). THE FISH CAN BE ENLARGED
TO ANY SIZE YOU LIKE BY USING A GRID (FIG. 1). BUT
WHATEVER THE SIZE, THE METHOD IS THE SAME FOR
ANY FISH WITH THE EXCEPTION OF FIN SIZES, THEIR
PLACEMENT & SHAPE. YOU COULD ACTUALLY MAKE
A CARVING OF A FISH YOU CAUGHT USING GOOD
PHOTOS AND MEASURING THE FISH.

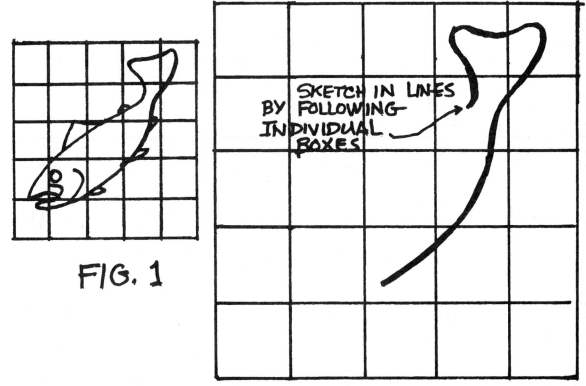

SKETCH IN LINES
BY FOLLOWING
INDIVIDUAL
BOXES

FIG. 1

STEP 2 • USING THE PATTERNS

TRANSFER BOTH THE TOP AND SIDE PATTERNS TO
HEAVY CARDBOARD AND CUT OUT THE SIDE VIEW
FIRST. LAY THE FISH ON ITS BACK AND HOLD THE
CARDBOARD ON TOP OF IT. DO NOT TRY TO BEND THE
CARDBOARD OVER THE FISH TO FIT THE CONTOURS.
THIS WILL ONLY CHANGE THE LENGTH OF YOUR
PATTERN. TRANSFER THE TOP VIEW BY FOL-
LOWING THE PATTERN SHAPE WITH A SHARP
PENCIL HELD AT RIGHT ANGLES TO THE PATTERN
EDGE (FIG. 2). HOLD THE PENCIL PERFECTLY
STRAIGHT UP AND DOWN.

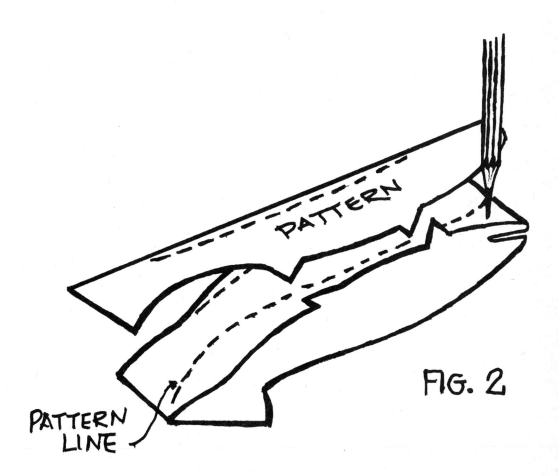

PATTERN

PATTERN LINE

FIG. 2

STEP 3 • SHAPING THE TOP OF THE BODY

IF YOU ALIGNED THE PATTERN WITH THE GRAIN ACCORDING TO THE PATTERN PAGE, YOU WILL FIND YOU WILL BE CARVING WITH THE GRAIN MOST OF THE TIME. USE A JACKKNIFE AND START CARVING AT THE BASE OF THE TAIL (FIG. 3). CARVE TOWARD THE HEAD WHILE ROUNDING SLIGHTLY (FIG.4). THIS ROUNDING CONTINUES FROM THE TOP OF THE DORSAL FIN TO THE PECTORAL FIN IN A SLIGHT ARC.

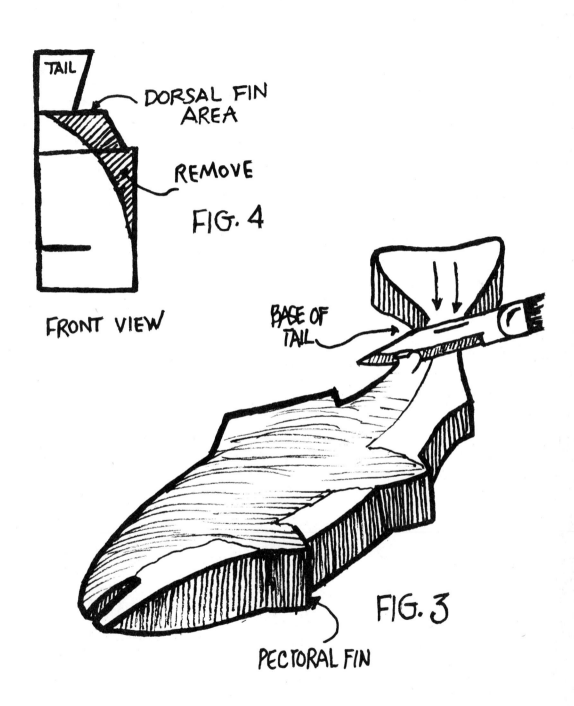

TAIL

DORSAL FIN AREA

REMOVE

FIG. 4

FRONT VIEW

BASE OF TAIL

FIG. 3

PECTORAL FIN

STEP 4. ROUNDING THE HEAD AND UNDERBODY

LEAVING THE TIP OF THE PECTORAL FIN WHERE IT IS, CARVE TOWARD THE HEAD SO YOU ARE CARVING AT AN ANGLE DOWN THE PECTORAL FIN AND ONTO THE UNDERBODY. ROUND THE HEAD COMPLETELY (FIG. 5). THE LOWER JAW WILL BE A LITTLE FLATTER THAN THE TOP OF THE HEAD. SKETCH IN THE TOP OF THE PECTORAL FIN AND CARVE FROM THE VENTRAL FIN TOWARD IT (FIG. 5A). YOU MAY FIND GRAIN CHANGES BETWEEN THE FINS. IF YOU DO, JUST REVERSE DIRECTION. GRAIN CHANGED FOR THIS FISH WHERE THE BLACK DOT IS (FIG. 5B). ALSO NOTE THAT THE VENTRAL FIN IS MUCH LOWER DOWN ON THE BODY THAN THE PECTORAL (FIG. 6).

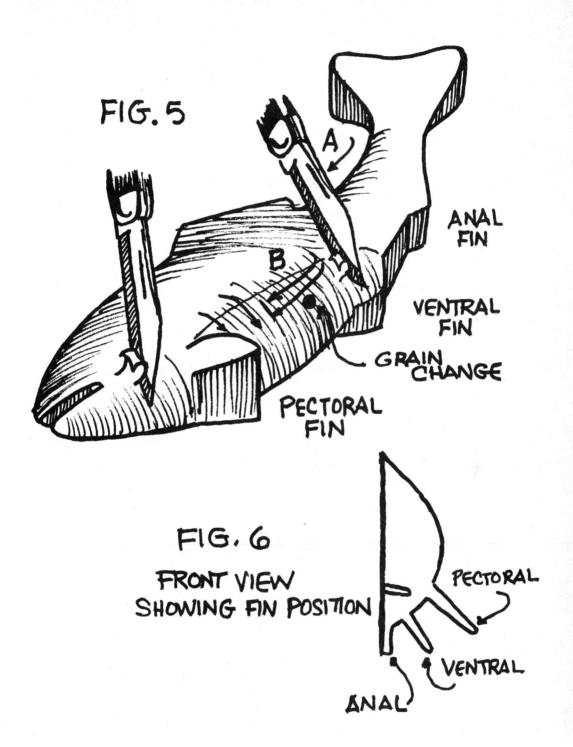

FIG. 5

ANAL
FIN

VENTRAL
FIN

GRAIN
CHANGE

PECTORAL
FIN

FIG. 6

FRONT VIEW
SHOWING FIN POSITION

PECTORAL

VENTRAL

ANAL

STEP 5 · CARVING THE BACKSIDE

AFTER A FEW STEPS, YOU MAY BE WONDERING WHY THE LITTLE FISH IN YOUR HANDS IS SO FAT. THE REASON BEHIND THIS IS TO GIVE THE TROUT A LITTLE MORE LIFE BY TWISTING THE BODY. REMEMBER THE TOP VIEW PATTERN'S DOTTED LINE THAT YOU DID NOT CUT ON. THIS WILL GIVE THE FISH ITS ARCED APPEARANCE. SKETCH IN THE LINES ON THE TROUT'S BACK AND BOTTOM BY USING THE PATTERN'S DOTTED LINE AND CARVE AWAY ALL SHADED AREAS FROM THE DORSAL FIN, TAIL, AND FINS ON THE BACK OF THE FISH (FIGS. 7 & 8). DO NOT CARVE AWAY THE ENTIRE BACKSIDE. CARVE ONLY ENOUGH TO SHOW A GOOD SHADOW WHEN IT'S PLACED AGAINST A FLAT SURFACE (FIG. 9).

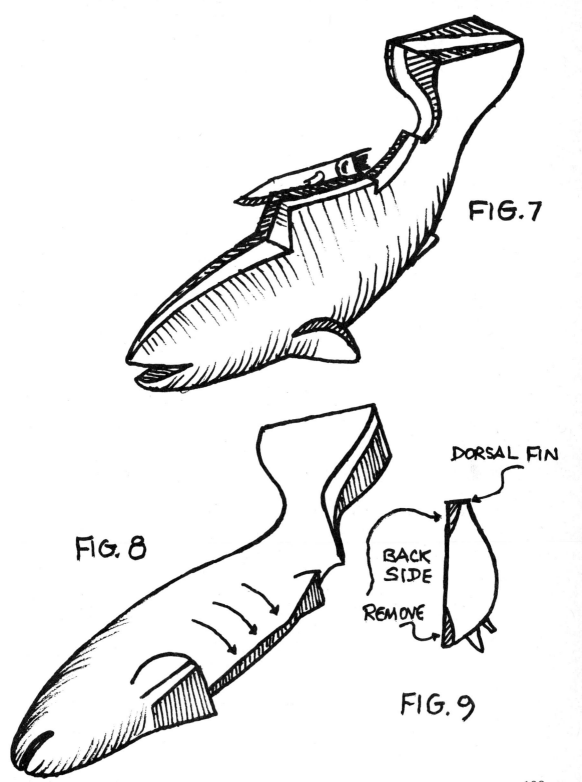

FIG. 7

FIG. 8

DORSAL FIN

BACK SIDE

REMOVE

FIG. 9

STEP 6. CARVING THE REMAINING FINS

TO CARVE THE DORSAL AND ADIPOSE FINS, SKETCH IN A LINE ALONG THE BASE OF THEM (FIG. 10), FOLLOWING THE CONTOUR OF THE BODY. WITH THE POINT OF THE JACKKNIFE, CUT STRAIGHT IN AT THE BASE OF BOTH FINS AND REMOVE WOOD, LEAVING THE FINS WITH THE ILLUSION OF BEING THIN AT THEIR TOPS (FIG. 11). REROUND THE TOP OF THE BODY IN THESE AREAS. BUT DO NOT CARVE THEM TOO THIN SINCE YOU WILL HAVE TO GO BACK AND PUT IN DETAILS. ALSO CARVE AWAY WOOD FROM THE BACKS OF THE FINS SO THEY DO NOT LOOK TOO THICK AND THAT THEY ARE OF UNIFORM THICKNESS.

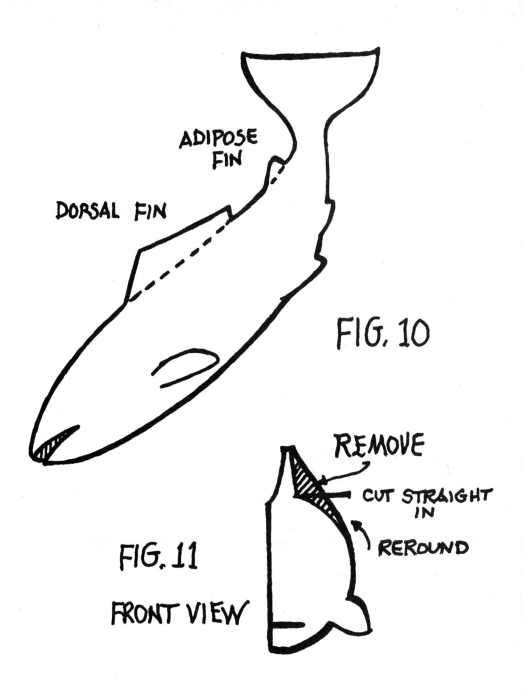

ADIPOSE FIN

DORSAL FIN

FIG. 10

REMOVE

CUT STRAIGHT IN

REROUND

FIG. 11

FRONT VIEW

STEP 7. SHAPING THE TAIL

WITH THE POINT OF YOUR JACKKNIFE, CUT STRAIGHT DOWN INTO THE BASE OF THE TAIL (FIG. 12A) TO FORM AN ARCED CUT. DO NOT GO TOO DEEP AS YOU MAY SEVER THE TAIL FROM THE BODY. THE OBJECT IS TO LOWER AND THIN THE TAIL (FIG. 12B & 13). SOFTEN THE AREA BY ROUNDING OVER THE RAISED BODY SECTION INTO THE TAIL (FIG. 13).

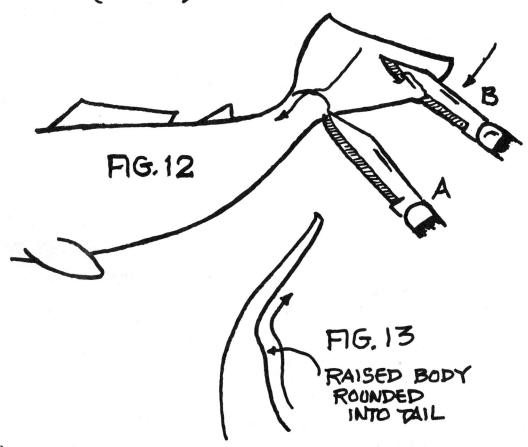

FIG. 12

FIG. 13
RAISED BODY
ROUNDED
INTO TAIL

STEP 8 · LOWERING THE FINS

CAREFULLY SHAVE THE BACK SIDE OF THE PEC-
TORAL FIN UNTIL IT HAS A THIN APPEARANCE.
LEAVE MORE BULK IN THE CENTER OF THE FIN FOR
STRENGTH, BUT MAKE ALL EDGES THIN.
THE VENTRAL FIN IS ALSO CARVED THIN AND
IT, LIKE THE PECTORAL, COMES OFF THE BODY AT
AN ANGLE (SEE FIG. 14 FOR THOSE ANGLES).
THE ANAL FIN IS DIRECTLY IN THE CENTER OF
THE UNDERSIDE AND GOES STRAIGHT DOWN
INSTEAD OF AT AN ANGLE.

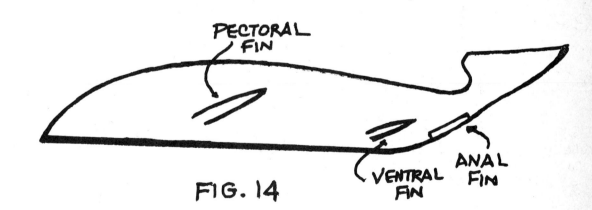

PECTORAL FIN

VENTRAL FIN

ANAL FIN

FIG. 14

STEP 9. FINISHING THE FINS

WITH A SMALL V PARTING TOOL, CARVE IN FIN LINES ON ALL FINS AND TAIL (FIG. 15). KEEP THE LINES AS CLOSE TOGETHER AS YOU CAN WITHOUT LEAVING FLAT AREAS BETWEEN YOUR CUT LINES. AFTER GROOVING, SAND THE ENTIRE PIECE EXCEPT FOR THE FINS AND TAIL.

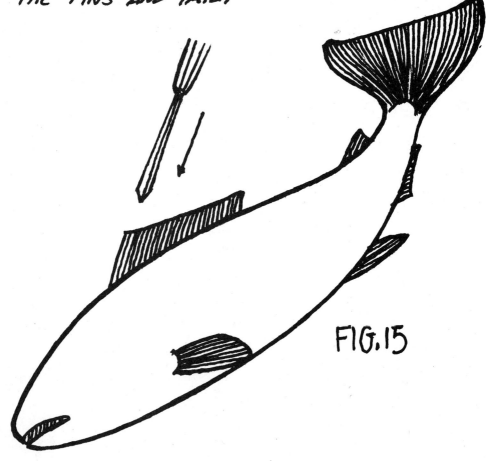

FIG. 15

STEP 10 · FINISHING THE HEAD

LOCATE THE GILLS AND CUT STRAIGHT DOWN ALONG THEM WITH THE JACKKNIFE. ALSO DEFINE THE EYE AND UPPER JAW COVER (FIGS. 16A, B, AND C). ROUND THE LIPS OVER TO GIVE THE MOUTH A DELICATE LOOK (FIG. 16D). CARVE AWAY WOOD FROM BEHIND THE GILLS AND JAW INTO THE EYE AND SHAPE (FIG. 17) SO THAT THE GILLS AND JAW APPEAR SLIGHTLY RAISED AND THE EYE IS DOME-SHAPED. SAND ALL AREAS SMOOTH. WITH A SMALL V PARTING TOOL, CUT THE GILL LINES (FIG. 16E).

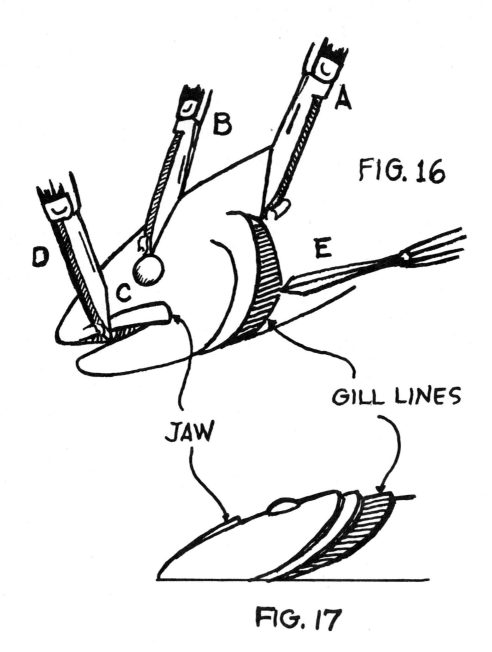

B

A

FIG. 16

D

C

E

GILL LINES

JAW

FIG. 17

STEP 11 • PAINT PREPARATION

AFTER A COMPLETE SANDING WITH FINE SAND-
PAPER, YOU ARE READY TO BEGIN PAINTING.
BECAUSE OF THE DIFFICULTY IN HOLDING THE
FISH WHILE PAINTING, GET A PIECE OF SCRAP
WOOD AND DRIVE NAILS THROUGH THE BACK OF
THE BOARD SO THE POINTS PROTRUDE (FIG. 18).
PRESS THE FISH ONTO THESE NAILS FIRMLY, BUT
NOT SO THE FISH IS TOUCHING THE BOARD.
THIS WILL MAKE PAINTING THE BACKS OF THE
FINS AND INSIDE THE MOUTH EASIER.

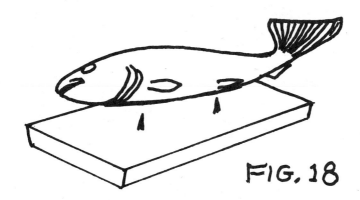

FIG. 18

STEP 12 · PAINTING WITH ACRYLICS

ACRYLICS ARE FAST DRYING PAINTS AND WORK EASILY. TRY USING GRUMBACHER HYPLAR ACRYLICS. THE COLORS SEEM QUITE GOOD. GIVE THE FISH A COMPLETE COAT OF TITANIUM WHITE EXCEPT FOR THE BACK. BRUSH THE PAINT ON EVENLY WITH AS FEW BRUSH MARKS AS POSSIBLE. THE FIRST COAT IS ONLY A BASE COAT AND WILL RAISE THE GRAIN SLIGHTLY. AFTER THE PAINT DRIES (5-10 MINUTES), CAREFULLY SAND THE WOOD SMOOTH WITH 120 GRIT SANDPAPER OR FINER. THE SMOOTHER THE FINISH ON THE BODY, THE WETTER THE FISH WILL APPEAR WHEN COMPLETED.

STEP 13 · MORE PAINTING

PAINT THE ENTIRE TROUT AGAIN WITH TITANIUM WHITE. FOR A GREENISH BROWN COLOR ON THE TOP OF THE FISH, MIX RAW SIENNA AND GREEN EQUALLY AND MIX WITH WHITE TO LIGHTEN. ADD A SMALL AMOUNT OF CADMIUM LIGHT YELLOW AND YOU SHOULD HAVE A GREENISH BROWN COLOR A LITTLE MORE ON THE BROWN SIDE. START AT THE TOP NEAR THE FINS ON THE BACK AND PAINT TOWARD THE MIDLINE (FIG. 19). AS YOU GET NEAR THE MIDLINE, LIGHTEN THE COLOR WITH WHITE. PAINT THE TAIL AND FINS ON THE BACK AND THE PECTORAL FIN WITH THIS COLOR LIGHTENED. AFTER THE PAINT DRIES, MIX THE SAME COLORS BUT A LITTLE DARKER AND REPEAT THE PROCESS. WHEN DRY, GIVE THE ENTIRE CARVING A COAT OF HIGH GLOSS POLYURETHANE.

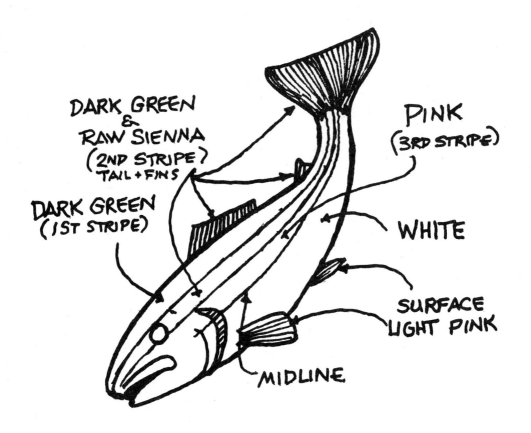

DARK GREEN
&
RAW SIENNA
(2ND STRIPE)
TAIL + FINS

DARK GREEN
(1ST STRIPE)

PINK
(3RD STRIPE)

WHITE

SURFACE
LIGHT PINK

MIDLINE

FIG. 19

STEP 14 • PAINTING THE SECOND COAT

SAND THE POLYURETHANE WITH EXTRA FINE SAND-PAPER (400 GRIT). YOU CAN NOW USE ENAMELS AND TINTING COLORS BECAUSE THEY BLEND MUCH BETTER THAN ACRYLICS AND GIVE YOU MORE TIME FOR BLENDING THE COLORS TOGETHER. FOR THE DARK GREEN STRIPE, TAKE DARK GREEN EN-AMEL AND THIN A BIT WITH TURPENTINE AND PAINT IN 1ST STRIPE AREA (FIG.19). THEN MIX DARK GREEN ENAMEL AND RAW SIENNA TINTING COLOR TOGETHER FOR THE SECOND STRIPE. MIX WHITE AND RED ENAMEL TO MAKE A PINK AND PAINT THE THIRD STRIPE, BLENDING THE PINK INTO THE PREVIOUS STRIPE. USE STRAIGHT WHITE ENAMEL FOR THE REMAINDER OF THE FISH AND BLEND THAT INTO THE PINK. BRUSH A SOFT PINK OVER THE LOWER FINS WHILE THE WHITE IS STILL WET. PAINT THE BACK FINS AND TAIL A DARK GREEN FIRST AND GO OVER IT WITH THE RAW SIENNA AND DARK GREEN MIX (FIG.19).

STEP 15 • FINAL PAINTING

WITH A FINELY POINTED BRUSH, PAINT A THIN WHITE STRIPE ALONG THE SIDE OF THE FISH WHERE THE PINK AND RAW SIENNA MIX COME TOGETHER (FIG. 20). PAINT A FINE WHITE LINE ALONG THE REAR EDGES OF THE GILL COVERS AND UPPER JAW. WITH A DRY BRUSH, BLEND WHITE INTO THE GILL COVERS BY BRUSHING TOWARD THE HEAD. MIX A GLOSS BLACK WITH A LITTLE RAW SIENNA AND PAINT SMALL DOTS ALL OVER THE TOP PART OF THE BODY (FIG. 20). MAKE THE DOTS LARGER TOWARD THE DORSAL FIN AND SMALLER TOWARD THE WHITE MIDLINE. ALSO DO THE TAIL WITH THESE DOTS. PAINT THE EYE YELLOW WITH A BLACK CENTER. PAINT THE GILLS RED AND STREAK THEM WITH BLACK.

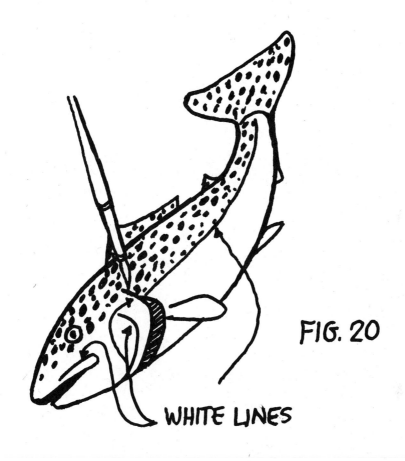

FIG. 20

WHITE LINES

STEP 16· BACKBOARD MOUNTING

THIS FISH MIGHT BE BEST MOUNTED ON A KNOT-FREE PIECE OF PINE WITH THE EDGE CHAMFERED AND SANDED. CUTTING THE OVAL FROM A PIECE OF BOARD MEASURING APPROXIMATELY 8"x14" WOULD BE BEST. THEN A GOLDEN OAK STAIN WILL GIVE CONTRAST TO THE FISH. PAINT THE CHAMFER A SATIN BLACK ENAMEL. TO MOUNT THE FISH, LAY IT ON THE FINISHED WOOD AND CENTER IT. WHERE THE FISH HAS THE MOST BULK, MARK FOR TWO HOLES. THE FISH IS BEST HELD WITH TWO 1" LONG BY ¼" DIAMETER DOWELS PUSHED INTO DRILLED HOLES ½" DEEP IN THE BACKBOARD. RUB PENCIL LEAD ON THE ENDS OF THE DOWELS AFTER THEY ARE MOUNTED AND GLUED INTO BOARD. BY PRESSING FISH ON DOWEL ENDS, MARKS WILL BE LEFT ON THE BACK OF THE FISH. DRILL APPROPRIATE HOLES ¼" DEEP INTO FISH'S BACK. WHEN MOUNTED, THE FISH SHOULD NOT BE TOUCHING THE BACKBOARD BUT SHOULD BE ¼" AWAY (FIG. 21). THIS WILL CREATE A SHADOW THAT WILL MAKE THE FISH SEEM FULLER.

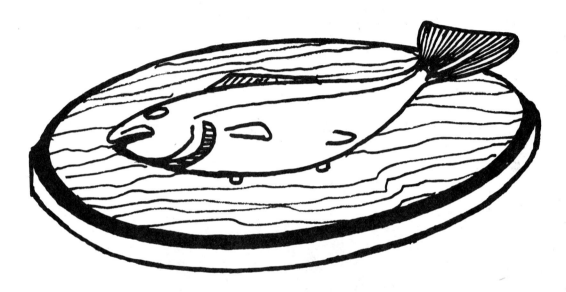

FIG. 21

Traditional
AMERICAN
EAGLE

TOOLS NEEDED

McCARTHY KNIFE

FISHTAIL GOUGE ⌣

JACKKNIFE

∨ PARTING TOOL ∨

Photo by Tad Goodale.

EAGLE PATTERN

ENLARGE BY USING GRID

ENLARGED PATTERNS
AVAILABLE

SEE APPENDIX
FOR ADDRESS

STEP 1. STARTING THE EAGLE

AFTER YOU HAVE TRANSFERRED YOUR PATTERN ONTO 2" THICK WOOD, A SINGLE PIECE OF KNOT-FREE BOARD (EASTERN WHITE PINE IS THE BEST CHOICE), BANDSAW THE EAGLE TO SHAPE. THEN SECURE IT TO A BACKBOARD. THIS CAN BE DONE WITH SPOTS OF HOT MELT GLUE OR SMALL SCREWS. TRY TO HAVE THE BACKBOARD GREATER THAN THE SIZE OF THE EAGLE SO THAT THE BOARD INSTEAD OF THE CARVING CAN BE CLAMPED. WITH A FISHTAIL GOUGE, CARVE FROM THE CROWNS OF THE WINGS, WORKING DOWN AND TAPERING THE WOOD TOWARD THE WINGTIPS (FIGS. 1 AND 2) TO A $\frac{1}{2}$" THICKNESS AT WINGTIPS.

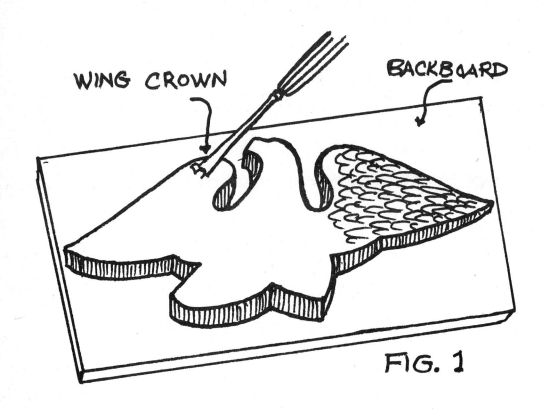

WING CROWN

BACKBOARD

FIG. 1

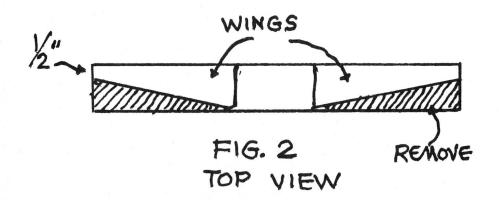

WINGS

1/2"

FIG. 2
TOP VIEW

REMOVE

STEP 2 • SHAPING THE BODY

IF YOU HAVEN'T DONE SO, SKETCH IN THE SHIELD AND FEET OF THE EAGLE. SKETCH A LINE ALONG THE TAIL ½" FROM THE BACKBOARD. SKETCH A SIMILAR LINE ALONG THE BOTTOM EDGES OF THE WINGS. CUT STRAIGHT DOWN AROUND THE FEET AND SHIELD WITH THE McCARTHY KNIFE AS A STOP CUT AND CARVE AWAY WOOD FROM AROUND THEM (FIG. 3), BUT AS YOU DO, ROUND THE BODY (FIG. 3 ARROWS). THEN REMOVE WOOD TO THE LINES ON THE WINGS AND TAIL EDGES. ALSO, THE HEAD AND WING CROWNS WILL HAVE TO BE MADE SLIGHTLY LOWER THAN THE SHIELD (FIG. 4). AS YOU DO THAT, ROUND THE NECK ON EACH SIDE.

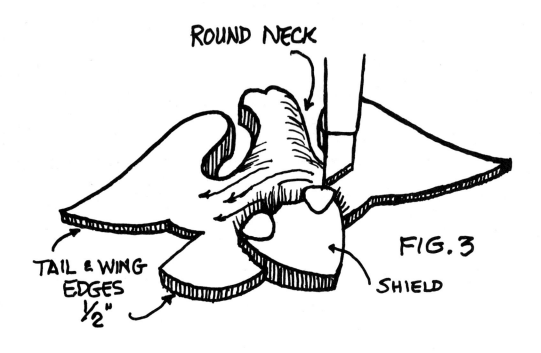

ROUND NECK

TAIL & WING
EDGES
½"

SHIELD

FIG. 3

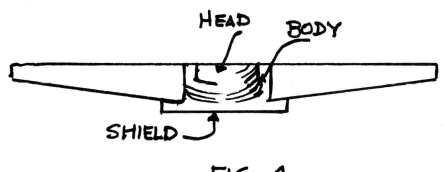

HEAD   BODY

SHIELD

FIG. 4
TOP VIEW

STEP 3. SHAPING THE SHIELD AND FEET

THE SHIELD WILL BE CONVEXLY SHAPED FROM SIDE TO SIDE AND FROM TOP TO BOTTOM (FIG. 5). START BY LOWERING THE SHIELD 1/4" BETWEEN AND BELOW THE FEET (FIG. 6). THEN CARVE AWAY WOOD FROM BOTH SIDES TO WITHIN 1/4" OF THE TAIL AND WINGS. THEN ROUND THE SHIELD FROM ITS TOP POINT UNTIL IT IS 1/2" FROM THE BACKBOARD (FIG. 5).

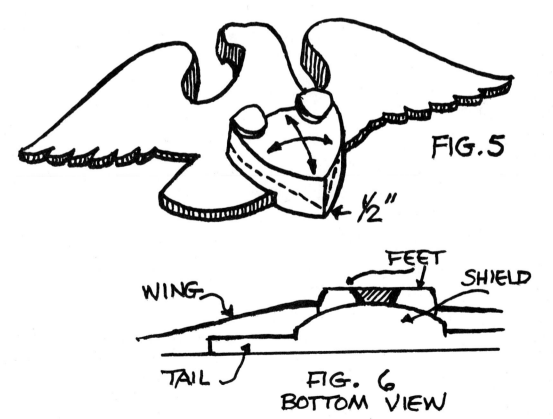

FIG. 5

1/2"

WING
FEET
SHIELD
TAIL
FIG. 6
BOTTOM VIEW

STEP 4· SHAPING THE WING CROWNS

SKETCH IN THE WING CROWN LINES, TAPERING THEM AS THEY APPROACH THE WING TIPS (FIG.7). BEGIN BY ROUNDING OVER THE WING CROWNS AS ILLUSTRATED IN FIG.8. THEN ROUND OVER TOWARD THE BACK OF THE WINGS (FIG.9). YOU MAY HAVE TO REMOVE THE EAGLE FROM THE BACKBOARD TO CUT AWAY WOOD. ALSO ROUND THE BACK OF THE HEAD SLIGHTLY ALONG THE BASE OF THE NECK AND ONTO THE BASE OF THE WINGS. THEN REMOVE WOOD FROM THE BACK OF THE HEAD TO GIVE THE EFFECT OF ITS BEING TURNED TOWARD THE FRONT (FIG.8).

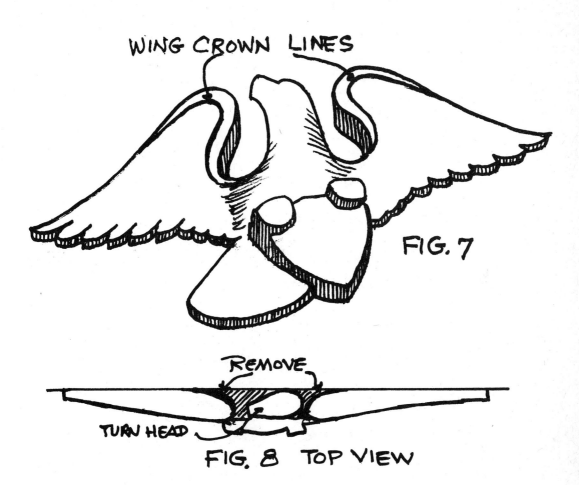

WING CROWN LINES

FIG. 7

REMOVE

TURN HEAD

FIG. 8 TOP VIEW

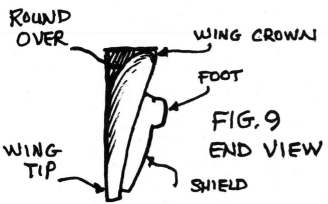

ROUND OVER

WING CROWN

FOOT

FIG. 9
END VIEW

WING TIP

SHIELD

STEP 5· MORE ON THE WINGS

WORKING FROM THOSE WING CROWN LINES, USE A FISHTAIL GOUGE AND CARVE A CONCAVE AREA, LEVELING OFF THE WOOD AS YOU'RE NEARING THE BOTTOM EDGES (FIG. 10A). CONTINUE THIS UNTIL THE CONCAVE AREA LOOKS LIKE THE POCKET OF A BASEBALL GLOVE (FIG. 10B). YOU CAN NOW DRAW THE INITIAL FEATHER LAYERS BY FOLLOWING THE PATTERN PAGE. SKETCH IN THE FIRST THREE FEATHERS AT THE WING CROWNS. YOU ARE NOT SKETCHING IN ALL FEATHERS BECAUSE YOU WILL BE LAYERING THESE IN STEPS. DOING ONE ROW, THEN, WOULD REMOVE THE LINES FROM THE NEXT ROW. WAIT TO SKETCH IN ROWS AFTER CARVING PRECEDING ROWS.

FIG. 10

STEP 6. FEATHERING THE EAGLE

USING THE McCARTHY KNIFE, CUT STRAIGHT DOWN AROUND THE THREE FEATHERS ON EACH WING (FIG. 11A). THIS IS ONLY A STOP CUT TO PREVENT CHIPPING AWAY THE FEATHERS. THEN WITH A FISHTAIL GOUGE (FIG. 11B), LOWER THE AREA JUST BELOW THE FEATHERS ABOUT 1/8". CARVE THEM SO THEY HAVE A SHINGLED LOOK. THEN SKETCH IN THE NEXT GROUPING OF FEATHERS FROM THE PATTERN DOWN ALONG THE INSIDE EDGES OF THE WINGS INTO THE BODY.

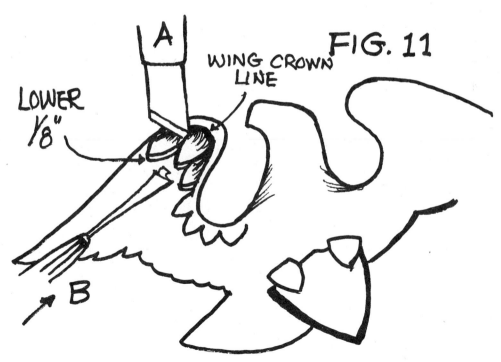

FIG. 11

A

WING CROWN LINE

LOWER 1/8"

B

STEP 7. COMPLETING THE WING FEATHERS

THE REMAINING SMALL FEATHERS ARE DONE AS DESCRIBED IN STEP 6. THE LONG FEATHERS (FIG. 12) HOWEVER, ARE DONE ONE AT A TIME, STARTING AT FEATHER 1. REMOVE ABOUT 1/8" OF WOOD FROM THE EDGE OF THAT FEATHER WITH THE KNIFE (FIG. 13A). AS YOU REMOVE THIS WOOD, CARVE FEATHER 2 CONCAVELY (FIG. 13B). THEN SKETCH IN THE OUTLINE OF FEATHER 2, MAKE A STOP CUT AROUND THAT, AND CARVE THE ADJOINING AREA CONCAVELY. DON'T FORGET TO GO BACK AND CARVE FEATHER 1 WITH A CONCAVE SHAPE (FIG. 13C).

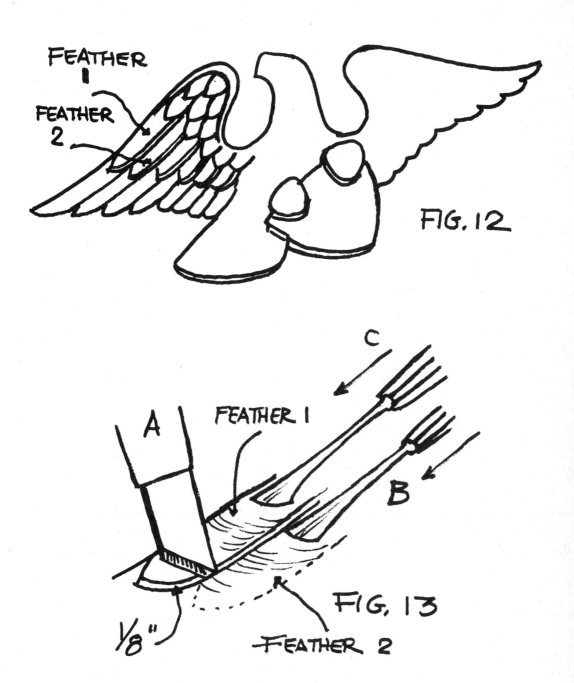

FEATHER 1

FEATHER 2

FIG. 12

C

A

FEATHER 1

B

1/8"

FIG. 13

FEATHER 2

STEP 8. SHAPING THE FEET

START BY ROUNDING OVER THE FEET FROM SIDE TO SIDE AND TOP TO BOTTOM. THEY MAY BE A BIT TOO HIGH OFF THE SHIELD, SO TRY TO GET THEM ONLY ¼" FROM THE SHIELD FACE BY FLATTENING THEM FIRST (FIG. 14A). SKETCH IN TWO LINES, BRINGING THEM ALMOST TOGETHER AT THE TALON AREA (FIG. 15). WITH THE KNIFE, CUT DEEP 'V's INTO THESE LINES (FIG. 14B) TO FORM THE THREE TOES OF THE FOOT. BRING THE TALON POINTS DOWN TO THE SURFACE OF THE SHIELD (FIG. 16 SIDE VIEW).

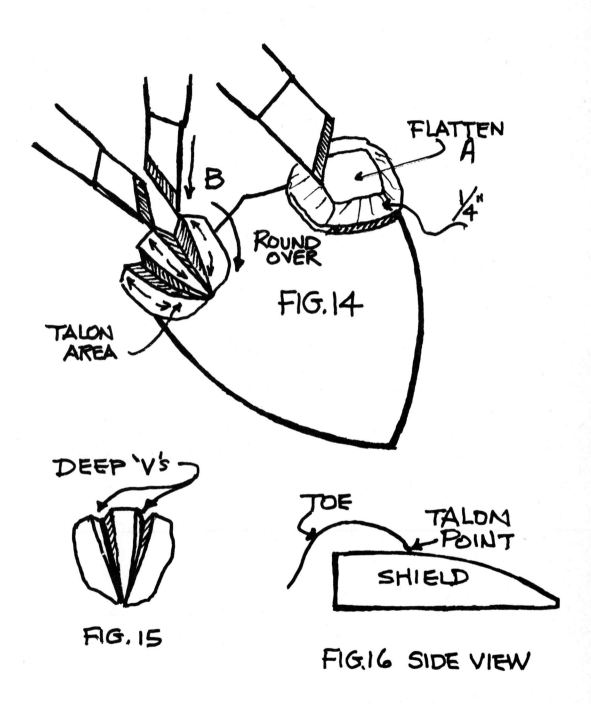

FLATTEN A

B

1/4"

ROUND OVER

FIG. 14

TALON AREA

DEEP 'V's

FIG. 15

TOE

TALON POINT

SHIELD

FIG. 16 SIDE VIEW

141

STEP 9 · FINISHING THE TOES AND TALONS

BY USING THE CENTER TALON AS A GUIDE FOR SIZE, CUT STRAIGHT DOWN ALONG THE OUTER EDGES OF THE OUTSIDE TOES, BRINGING THEIR POINTS TOGETHER (FIG. 17). CUT THESE WITH A SLIGHT ARC. THE DIFFICULTY IN MAKING TOES IS GETTING THEM THE SAME SIZE AND SHAPE. BUT ONCE YOU HAVE THEM EQUAL, ROUND OVER EACH TALON FROM SIDE TO SIDE. CUT A 'V' ALONG THE TALON LINES AND LOWER THEM FROM THE TOES SLIGHTLY (FIG. 18A). IF YOU WORK CAREFULLY WITH A JACKKNIFE, YOU CAN CUT A SMALL PIECE FROM UNDER EACH TALON TO MAKE IT LOOK MORE POINTED (FIG. 18B). FINALLY, SAND THE TALONS AND TOES.

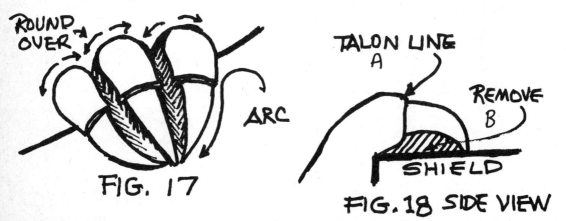

ROUND OVER

ARC

FIG. 17

TALON LINE
A

REMOVE
B

SHIELD

FIG. 18 SIDE VIEW

STEP 10 · WORKING ON THE BODY AND TAIL

USING THE PATTERN AS A GUIDE, CUT STRAIGHT IN AT A SLIGHT ANGLE TO MARK THE BROW (FIG. 19). CUT ALONG THE EYE LINE AND LOWER THE FACE AND NECK FROM THE EYE. THIS WILL GIVE YOU ROOM TO ROUND THE EYE (FIG. 19). AS YOU LOWER THE NECK, SMOOTH AND ROUND THE BEAK. MAKE A CLEAN SHARP 'V' TO FORM THE MOUTH WHILE AT THE SAME TIME BRINGING THE BEAK'S TIP TO A POINT (FIG. 20A). MAKE A SMALL, CONCAVE, HALF-ROUNDED CUT INTO THE EYE TO FORM THE PUPIL (FIG. 20B). BEFORE YOU CARVE THE BODY FEATHERS, MAKE SURE THE BODY IS LOWERED EVENLY WITH A SLIGHTLY ROUNDED SHAPE. AS YOU DRAW ON THE BODY FEATHERS, MAKE SURE THEY HAVE AN ARCED PATTERN AS THEY NEAR THE TAIL (FIG. 20C). THIS ESTABLISHES THE DIFFERENCE BETWEEN BODY AND TAIL. LOWER ALL BODY FEATHERS AS YOU DID IN STEP 6. BLEND THE BODY FEATHERS INTO THE WING FEATHERS SO THEY MEET WITH →

STEP 10 · CONTINUED

NO FLAT OR EMPTY AREAS (FIG. 20D). LAYER THE TAIL FEATHERS FROM BOTH SIDES INTO THE MIDDLE. THEN NOTCH THE ENDS OF THE TAIL FEATHERS AND MAKE SURE ALL SAW MARKS ARE CARVED AWAY (FIG. 20E).

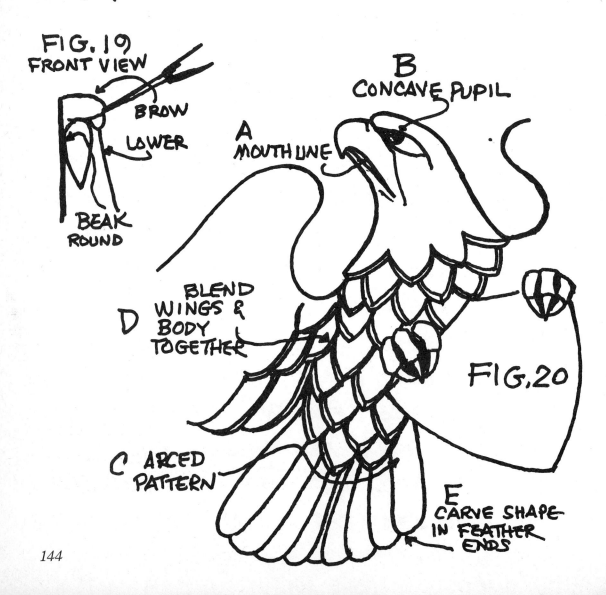

FIG. 19
FRONT VIEW

BROW

LOWER

BEAK
ROUND

B
CONCAVE PUPIL

A
MOUTH LINE

D
BLEND
WINGS &
BODY
TOGETHER

FIG. 20

C ARCED
PATTERN

E
CARVE SHAPE
IN FEATHER
ENDS

STEP 11 · BACK TO THE SHIELD

CUT A SHALLOW 'V' WITH THE POINT OF THE McCARTHY KNIFE AROUND THE PERIMETER OF THE SHIELD, LEAVING A 1/8" EDGE (FIG. 21A). DON'T TRY TO DO THIS WITH A V PARTING TOOL BECAUSE THE GRAIN WILL BREAK AWAY. CUT TWO 'V' LINES ACROSS THE SHIELD, LEAVING A 1/8" SPACE BETWEEN THEM (FIG. 21B). SKETCH IN THREE STARS ACROSS THE SHIELD'S TOP, KEEPING THEM IN LINE. THE TWO OUTSIDE STARS WILL BE PARTIALLY HIDDEN BY THE CLAWS (FIG. 21). CUT STRAIGHT DOWN WITH THE POINT OF THE KNIFE INTO THE CENTER OF EACH STAR AND CUT OUTWARD TO EACH POINT (FIG. 22A). REMOVE WOOD AT AN ANGLE, FOLLOWING THE ARROWS IN FIG. 22 TO KEEP WITH THE GRAIN (FIG. 22B). YOUR STAR SHOULD LOOK LIKE THAT IN FIG. 23 WITH THE DEEPEST PART BEING AT ITS CENTER. SKETCH IN THE LINES FOR THE 13 STRIPES AND CUT A SHARP 'V' ON EACH LINE TO SEPARATE THE STRIPES.

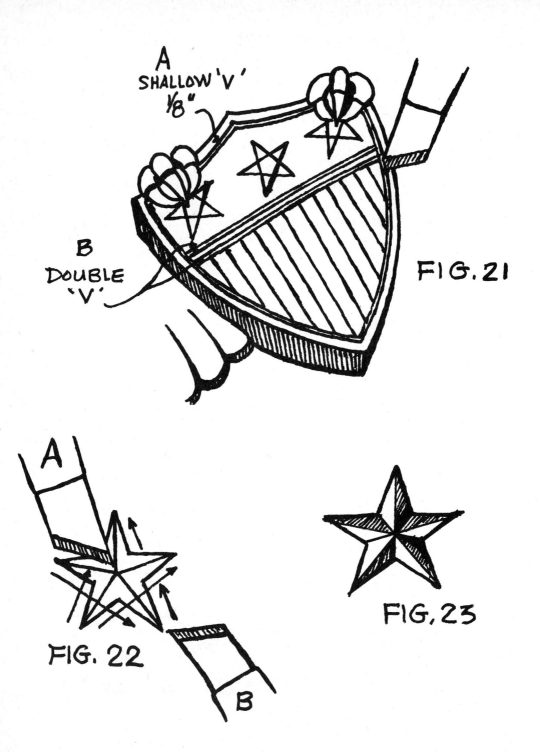

A
SHALLOW 'V'
1/8"

B
DOUBLE
'V'

FIG. 21

A

B

FIG. 22

FIG. 23

146

STEP 12. FEATHER SPLITS

ON MOST TRADITIONAL EAGLES, THE WOODCARVER CUTS IN RANDOM FEATHER SPLITS SO THE FEATHERS DO NOT LOOK SMOOTH. USE A 'V' PARTING TOOL AND CUT A DOUBLE 'V' DOWN ALL FEATHERS, TAPERING THEM AS YOU NEAR THEIR ENDS. ON THE SMALL FEATHERS, THE DOUBLE 'V' IS DOWN THE CENTERS. ON THE LONGER ONES, HOWEVER, THE CUTS ARE OFFSET, GOING INTO THE POINTED ENDS (FIGS. 24A AND 25A).

MAKE SMALL SINGLE CUTS AT RANDOM ON THE SIDES OF THE FEATHERS (FIGS. 24B AND 25B). CUT TWO TO FOUR CUTS INTO EACH FEATHER. USE FIG. 26 FOR SUGGESTED CUTS.

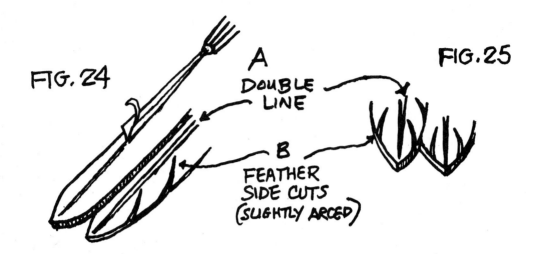

FIG. 24

FIG. 25

A
DOUBLE
LINE

B
FEATHER
SIDE CUTS
(SLIGHTLY ARCED)

FIG. 26

FEATHER SPLITS

STEP 13 · FINISHING THE EAGLE

STAIN THE ENTIRE EAGLE, FRONT AND BACK, WITH A WALNUT STAIN. SEAL THE ENTIRE PIECE WITH SATIN FINISH POLYURETHANE, GIVING IT THREE TO FOUR COATS. YOU CAN LEAVE THE EAGLE AS IS OR GOLD LEAF IT. BUT WHICHEVER YOU CHOOSE, YOU SHOULD PAINT THE SHIELD. USING ENAMELS, MAKE THE STARS WHITE AND THEIR BACKGROUND BLUE. MAKE THE STRIPES RED AND WHITE, STARTING WITH RED ON THE OUTSIDE. THE TRIM AND CROSS TRIM SHOULD BE GOLD. PAINT THE EYE WHITE AND THE PUPIL BLUE. USE RED FOR THE MOUTH. FINALLY, IF THEY ARE NOT GOLD-LEAFED, PAINT THE TOES GOLD. THE EAGLE IS NOW READY TO BE MOUNTED.

the WALL CLOCK
and Knickknack Shelf

TOOLS
NEEDED

McCARTHY KNIFE
FISHTAIL GOUGE

⌣

FLAT CHISEL

▬

151

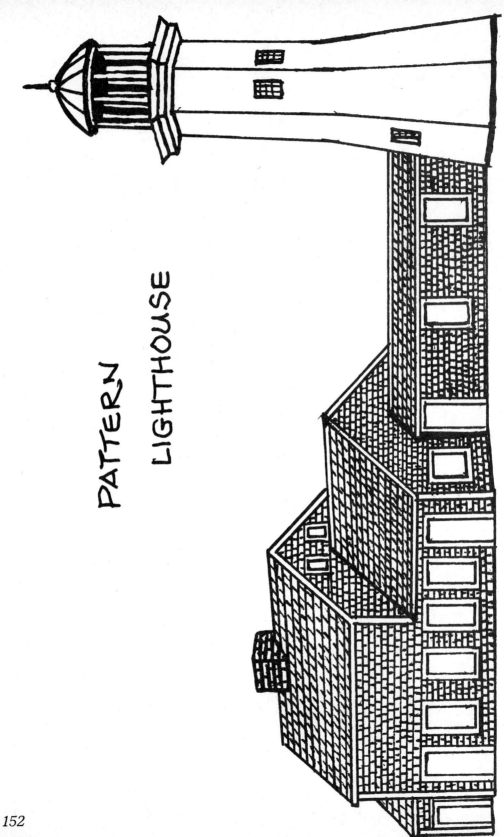

PATTERN LIGHTHOUSE

PATTERNS

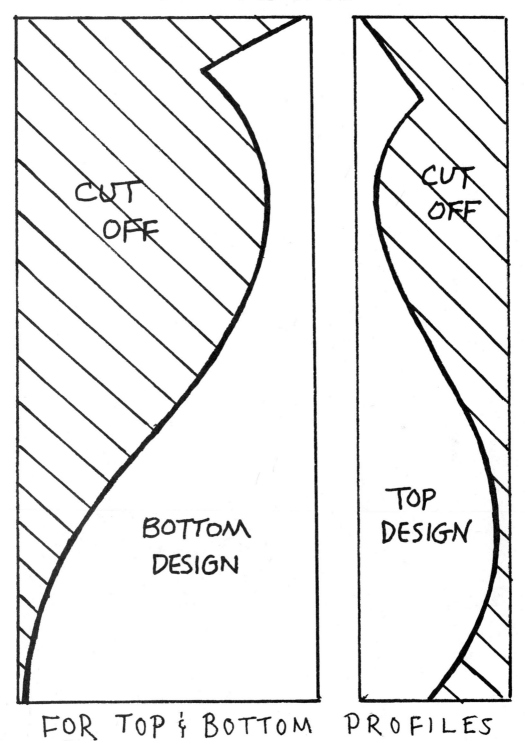

CUT
OFF

BOTTOM
DESIGN

CUT
OFF

TOP
DESIGN

FOR TOP & BOTTOM PROFILES

STEP I · GETTING STARTED

THIS IS A LOW RELIEF CARVING THAT HAS PERSPECTIVE ACCOMPLISHED BY MAKING SHARP CUTS WITH THE McCARTHY KNIFE. THE INSTRUCTIONS IN FACT SHOULD GIVE YOU ENOUGH KNOWLEDGE TO CARVE ANY BUILDING, INCLUDING YOUR OWN HOUSE, WHICH COULD BE AN INTERESTING PROJECT LATER ON.

YOU WILL HAVE TO GLUE UP TWO OR THREE PIECES OF 3/4" THICK PINE GIVEN THE DIMENSIONS IN FIG.1. IT ALSO SHOWS HOW BEST TO CLAMP THE BOARDS AND REVERSE THE GRAIN TO MINIMIZE WARPING. (FIG. 1A).

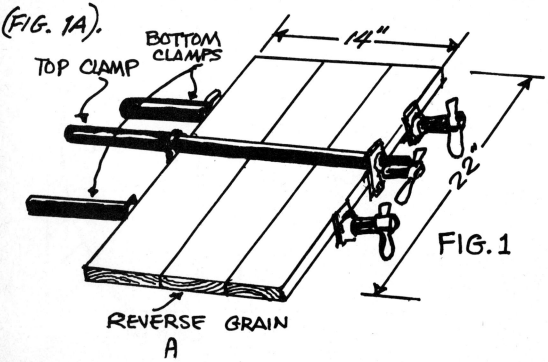

TOP CLAMP

BOTTOM CLAMPS

14"

2"

FIG.1

REVERSE GRAIN
A

STEP 2. TRANSFERRING THE TOP AND BOTTOM DESIGNS
AFTER THE GLUE HAS SET AND YOU HAVE SANDED THE
WOOD, DRAW A CENTERLINE DOWN THE LENGTH OF THE
PANEL. TRACE THE PATTERNS FROM THE BOOK AND
LAY THEM OUT, TOP AND BOTTOM. THEN REVERSE THEM
FOR THE OPPOSITE SIDE.

STEP 3 · LAYING OUT THE DIAL

MEASURE DOWN 6" FROM THE TOP OF THE PANEL AND
5" IN FROM THE SIDE FOR THE CENTER OF THE CLOCK
FACE (FIG. 2). WITH A SMALL COMPASS, DRAW A CIRCLE
8" IN DIAMETER (FIG. 2A). DRAW ANOTHER CIRCLE
1/4" INSIDE THE FIRST CIRCLE (FIG. 3). DIVIDE THE
CIRCLE INTO QUARTERS AND DIVIDE EACH QUARTER INTO
THIRDS. THESE WILL MAKE THE TWELVE POINTS OF THE
TIMEPIECE. YOU SHOULD FIND THE SPACES ALONG THE
CIRCUMFERENCE WILL BE ABOUT 2" APART. AGAIN WITH
THE COMPASS, DRAW ANOTHER CIRCLE 4" IN DIAMETER
(FIG. 4) INSIDE THE LARGER CIRCLE. THIS WILL BE THE
GUIDE FOR LAYING OUT THE POINTERS. TRANSFER THE
POINTERS IN FIGS. 5 AND 6 TO THE CLOCK FACE AS
SHOWN IN FIG. 4. LAST, LOCATE THE LIGHTHOUSE 7½"
FROM THE BOTTOM AND CENTER IT (FIG. 2B).

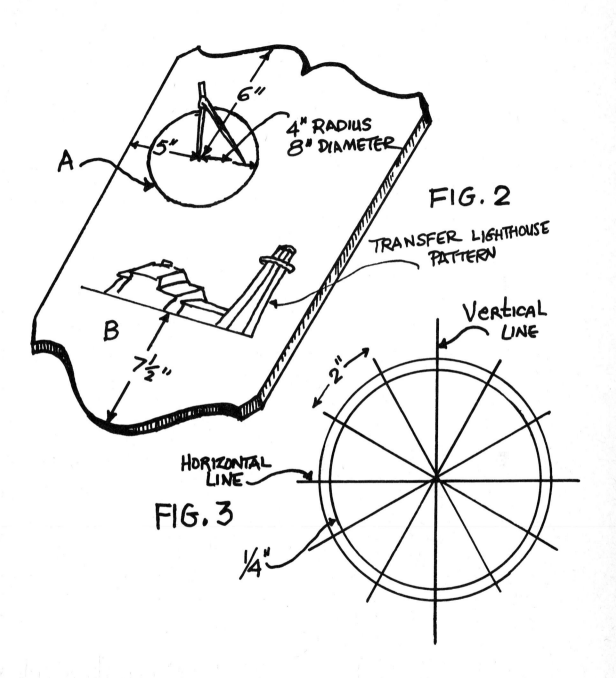

6"

4" RADIUS
8" DIAMETER

5"

A

FIG. 2

TRANSFER LIGHTHOUSE
PATTERN

B

7½"

VERTICAL
LINE

2"

HORIZONTAL
LINE

FIG. 3

¼"

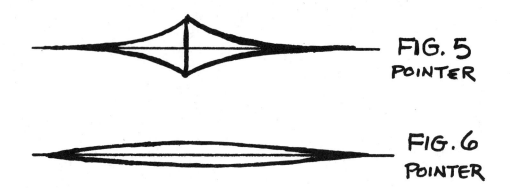

FIG. 5
POINTER

FIG. 6
POINTER

FIG. 4

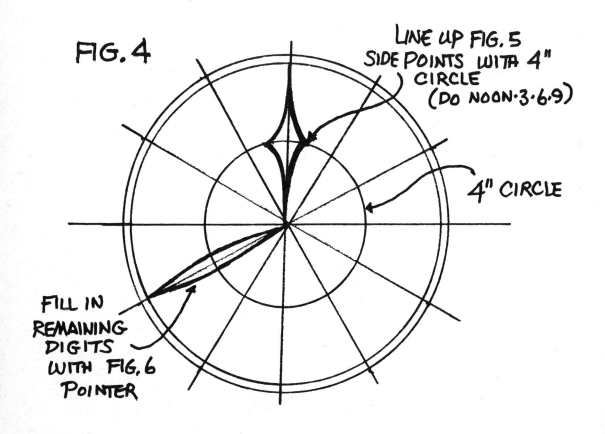

LINE UP FIG. 5
SIDE POINTS WITH 4"
CIRCLE
(DO NOON·3·6·9)

4" CIRCLE

FILL IN
REMAINING
DIGITS
WITH FIG. 6
POINTER

STEP 4. CARVING THE DIAL

START THE DIAL BY CARVING THE 3·6·9·12 POINTERS. START BY CUTTING ACROSS THE POINTED SIDES (FIG. 7). USING THE POINT OF THE McCARTHY KNIFE, CUT AT AN ANGLE USING THE ARROW DIRECTIONS GIVEN IN FIG. 7. WHEN FINISHED, YOUR CUTS SHOULD LOOK LIKE THOSE IN FIG. 8A. CUT THE REMAINING POINTERS USING THE ARROWS FOR A GUIDE IN FIG. 8, BUT BEFORE YOU START TO REMOVE WOOD, CUT A STRAIGHT LINE DOWN THE CENTERS AS A STOP CUT (FIG. 8B). THE 3-6-9-12 POINTERS SHOULD, WHEN FINISHED, BE CARVED INTO A CRISP 'V' (FIG. 9). TO DO THE PERIMETER, USE THE POINT OF THE KNIFE AND CUT A 'V' 1/4" WIDE ON THE TWO OUTSIDE CIRCLES BY FOLLOWING THE ARROWS IN FIG. 8C.

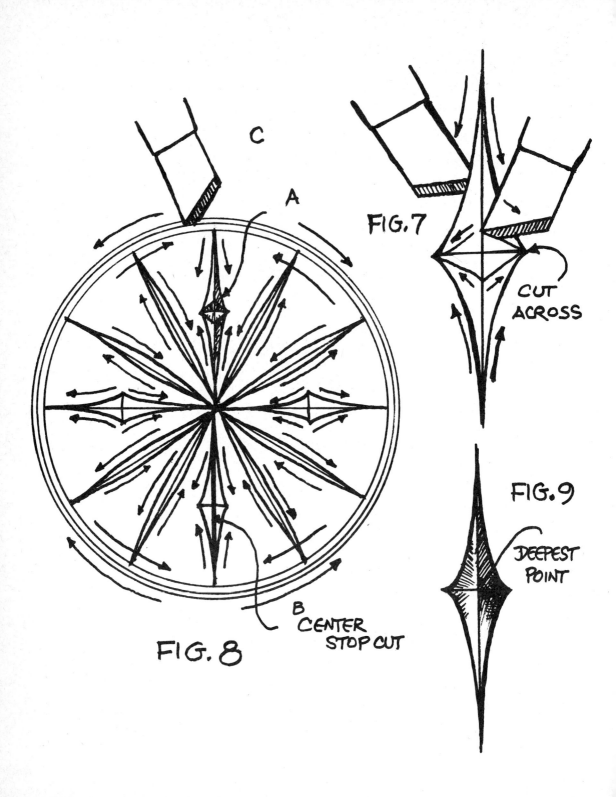

C

A

FIG. 7

CUT
ACROSS

B
CENTER
STOP CUT

FIG. 8

FIG. 9

DEEPEST
POINT

STEP 5 · STARTING THE LIGHTHOUSE

WITH THE POINT OF THE KNIFE, CUT PERFECTLY STRAIGHT DOWN AND AROUND THE ENTIRE LIGHT-HOUSE WITH EXCEPTION OF THE BASE OF THE BUILDINGS (FIG. 10). CUT AT AN ANGLE WITH THE KNIFE INTO THE FIRST CUT (FIG. 10A). REMOVE WOOD TO A 1/4" DEPTH. NEXT, BY LAYING THE KNIFE ALMOST FLAT (FIG. 10B) AND BY ROUGHLY FOLLOWING THE BACKGROUND LINE (FIG. 10C), YOU CAN SHAVE AWAY MUCH OF THE BACKGROUND SMOOTHLY WITH A GENTLE ROLL OF THE KNIFE INTO THE BUILDINGS (FIG. 11). THIS WILL GIVE YOU ROOM TO CARVE THE PERSPECTIVE OF THE LIGHTHOUSE.

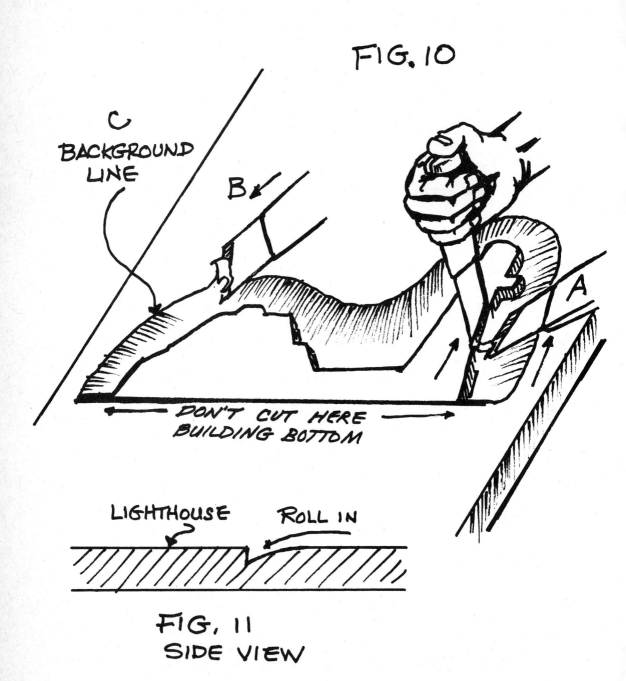

FIG. 10

C
BACKGROUND
LINE

B

A

DON'T CUT HERE
BUILDING BOTTOM

LIGHTHOUSE   ROLL IN

FIG. 11
SIDE VIEW

STEP 6 · SHAPING THE BUILDINGS

CUT A NARROW 'V' ALONG THE BOTTOM OF THE BUILD-INGS (DARK LINE FIG. 10) ABOUT 1/8" DEEP. CUT A 'V' ALONG THE UPPER AND LOWER EDGES OF THE TOWER COLLAR (FIG. 12 DARK LINES). CUT STRAIGHT DOWN TO SEPARATE BUILDING 1 AND LOWER IT FLATLY SO IT IS ONE HALF THE DEPTH OF THE BACK-GROUND. SEE FIG. 13 FOR THE SHAPE AND THE ANGLES. THIS ALLOWED ROOM TO CARVE THE TOWER. SINCE THE TOWER COLLAR PROTRUDES FROM THE TOWER, THE MAIN STRUCTURE MUST BE DROPPED BACK SLIGHTLY JUST BELOW THE COLLAR. ALSO, THE TOWER IS THICKER AT THE BOTTOM THAN NEAR ITS TOP (SEE FIG. 14). CARVE AWAY AT THE TOWER BY LAYING THE KNIFE FLAT AND CARVING FROM THE BOTTOM UP (FIG. 12A). IT WOULD HELP TO SKETCH IN THE TOWER FACETS BEFORE YOU START (FIG. 12B). THE TOWER TOP HAS FOUR FACETS (FIG. 15). BUT HERE YOU WILL HAVE TO ROUND OVER THE FACETS AS YOU REACH THE TOP OF THE DOME.

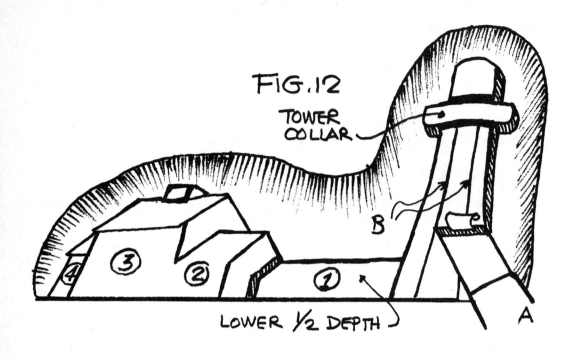

FIG.12

TOWER COLLAR

B

A

LOWER ½ DEPTH

FIG.13 BOTTOM VIEW

TOWER

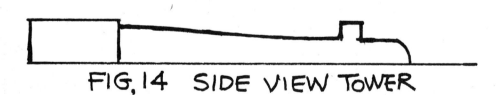

FIG.14 SIDE VIEW TOWER

FIG.15 TOWER
TOP VIEW

STEP 7. MORE ON THE TOWER TOP

CUT STRAIGHT DOWN ALONG THE BOTTOM OF THE TOWER CROWN AND LOWER THE WINDOW AREA 1/16", LEAVING A TINY EAVE (FIG. 16A). TO ESTABLISH CRISP ANGLES ON THE FACETS OF THE CROWN, CUT STRAIGHT DOWN ALONG THE FACET EDGES WITH THE POINT OF THE KNIFE (FIG. 16B). THIS IS ONLY TO MARK THEM. SKETCH IN THE WINDOWS, LEAVING THE CASINGS AROUND THEM. WITH THE POINT OF THE KNIFE, CUT STRAIGHT DOWN AROUND THE WINDOWS AND REMOVE SMALL 'V'S FROM THEIR SIDES. REMOVE CORNERS FROM THE TOWER COLLAR FOLLOWING THE SAME ANGLE AS THE TOWER'S BODY (FIG. 16C). CHECK THAT DISTANCE FROM THE COLLAR EDGE TO THE BODY TO BE SURE IT IS EQUAL. NEXT, DIVIDE THE THICKNESS OF THE COLLAR IN HALF ALONG ITS LENGTH AND LOWER THE BOTTOM HALF WITH AN ANGLE CUT (FIG. 17).

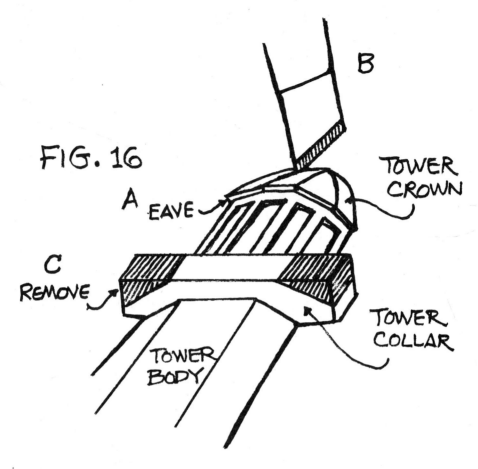

FIG. 16

B

TOWER CROWN

A EAVE

C REMOVE

TOWER COLLAR

TOWER BODY

FIG. 17

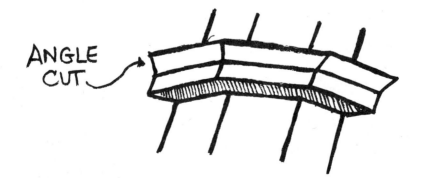

ANGLE CUT

STEP 8 · SHAPING THE BUILDINGS

BY LAYING THE KNIFE FLAT, CARVE AT AN ANGLE INTO THE ROOF OF BUILDING ① (FIGS. 18A AND 19). CARVE THE ROOF INTO THE BACKGROUND. TRY TO KEEP THE ANGLE WHERE THE SIDE AND ROOF COME TOGETHER AS CRISP AS POSSIBLE. FOR CARVING THE END OF BUILDING ②, CARVE STRAIGHT DOWN TOWARD THE BASE, STARTING YOUR FIRST CUT AS CLOSE TO BUILDING ① AS POSSIBLE AND SLOWLY FLATTEN THE ENTIRE END AT AN ANGLE (FIGS. 18B AND 20). TO ACHIEVE THE PROPER PERSPECTIVE, YOU WILL HAVE TO FLATTEN A SURFACE AREA SLIGHTLY LARGER THAN THE ACTUAL BUILDING END (FIG. 18 SHADED AREA).

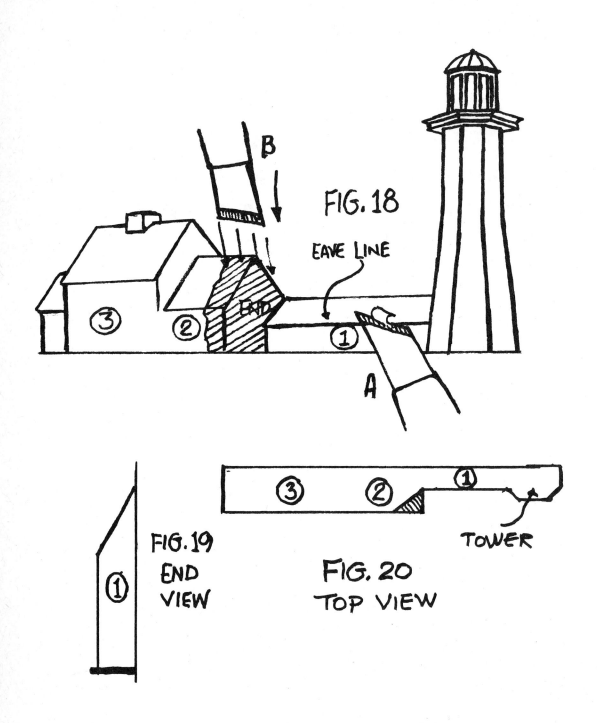

B

FIG. 18

EAVE LINE

END

③ ② ① A

FIG. 19
END
VIEW

①

③ ② ① TOWER

FIG. 20
TOP VIEW

STEP 9 · SHAPING BUILDINGS (CONTINUED)

TO CARVE THE END OF BUILDING ③, REPEAT THE SAME PROCEDURES YOU USED FOR ②. BUT BEFORE YOU START CARVING THE END ANGLE, CUT A 'V' ALONG THE ROOF LINE OF ② AND ③ (FIG. 21 DARK LINE). AGAIN, YOU WILL HAVE TO FLATTEN THE END OF ③ PAST ITS EAVE LINE. DO THE SAME CUT FOR THE CHIMNEY. NOTE THAT ALL THESE ANGLE CUTS SHOULD HAVE THE SAME PERSPECTIVE FOR THE BUILDINGS TO LOOK RIGHT.

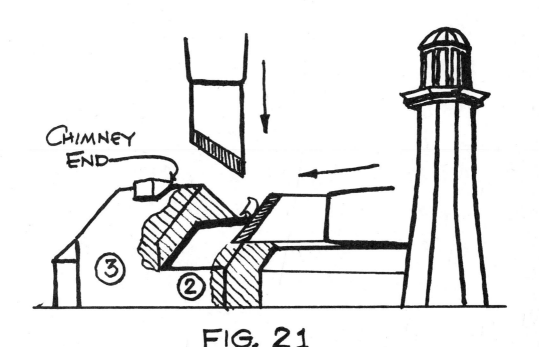

FIG. 21

STEP 10. FLATTENING THE ROOFS

SKETCH IN THE ROOF AND CORNER LINES (FIG. 22). THIS WHOLE AREA MUST BE FLATTENED BY LAYING THE KNIFE ALMOST FLAT TO THE SURFACE AND GRADUALLY SHAVING THE AREA DOWN SO THE FACING SIDE IS SLIGHTLY LOWER THAN THE BASE LINE. START AT THE CORNER OF BUILDING ② AND PUSH THE KNIFE ALONG (FIG. 22A). AS YOU REDUCE THIS AREA, YOU WILL HAVE TO CARVE AWAY SOME OF THE ROOF. THE LIGHTHOUSE BUILDINGS SHOULD LOOK LIKE THOSE IN FIG. 23. THE OBJECT OF THIS FLATTENING IS TO MAKE THE FIRST CORNER AS CRISP AND AS STRAIGHT AS POSSIBLE. SKETCH IN THE ROOF LINES AGAIN AND CARVE THEM FLAT, GOING TOWARD THE BACKGROUND. START AT THE EAVES AND MAKE THE OUTSIDE EDGES AS STRAIGHT AND AS CRISP AS POSSIBLE. REPEAT THE ROOF SHAPING AT THE SAME ANGLE. ON THE MAIN ROOF, SKIP THE CHIMNEY. FOR THE SMALL LEFT-END BUILDING, RELIEVE IT A LITTLE FROM BUILDING →

STEP 10 • CONTINUED

③ AND FLATTEN IT. THEN CARVE BACK THE ROOF. TO CARVE THE CHIMNEY, SIMPLY REDUCE ITS FACE AT THE SAME PLANE AS ALL OTHER SURFACES UNTIL YOU REACH THE ANGLED ROOF.

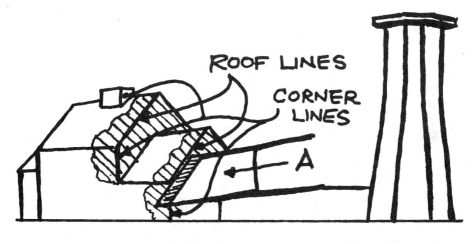

FIG. 22

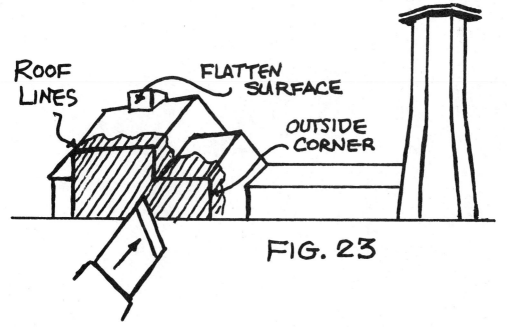

FIG. 23

STEP 11 · FINISHING TOUCHES

BY USING THE DETAILS ON THE PATTERN PAGE, SKETCH
IN ALL WINDOW AND DOOR CASINGS (FIGS. 24 AND 25),
THEN ALL CORNER BOARDS AND SHINGLES. START AT
THE TOWER WINDOWS AND, WITH A SMALL, FLAT CHISEL,
REMOVE ABOUT 1/8" FROM THE WINDOW AREA (FIG. 26A).
MOVE ON TO BUILDING ① AND WITH THE POINT OF
THE KNIFE, CUT STRAIGHT DOWN ALONG ALL BUILD-
ING TRIM (FIG. 26). ALL YOU ARE DOING IS
MAKING A SHALLOW STOP CUT. ALSO, BUILDING ①
IS THE ONLY BUILDING THAT HAS A SADDLE BOARD.
THIS CAN BE MADE WITH A STOP CUT. NEXT, CUT
STRAIGHT IN AROUND THE DOOR AND WINDOW CAS-
INGS AND TRIM BOARDS (SEE FIG. 24A). SCORE
THE SHINGLES (ROWS) BY FIRST CUTTING HORIZ-
ONTAL LINES (FIG. 27). NEXT, SKETCH IN THE
INDIVIDUAL SHINGLES BY STAGGERING THEM
(ALSO FIG. 27). TO MAKE THEM, INSERT THE POINT
OF THE KNIFE AND ROCK IT BACK AND FORTH (FIG. 28).
DO THE CHIMNEY IN THE SAME FASHION, BUT MAKE
SMALLER CUTS FOR THE BRICKS. SAND ALL SURFACES→

STEP 11. CONTINUED

AND EDGES, ROUNDING THE OUTSIDE EDGES SLIGHTLY.
DO NOT SAND THE LIGHTHOUSE TOWER.

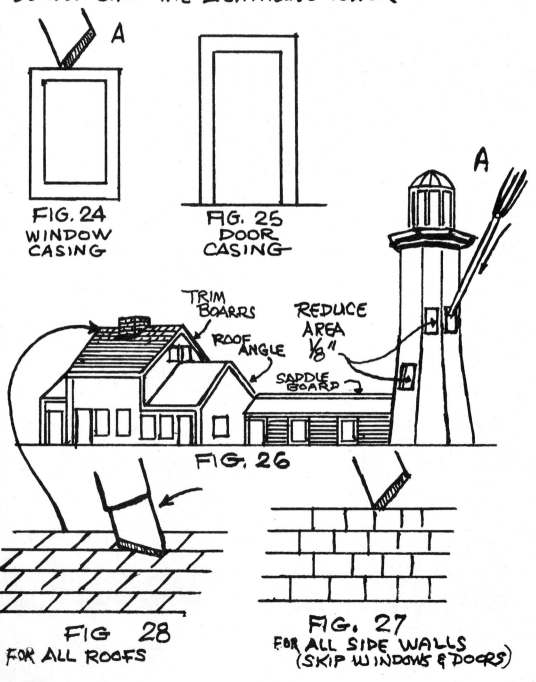

FIG. 24
WINDOW
CASING

FIG. 25
DOOR
CASING

TRIM
BOARRS

ROOF
ANGLE

REDUCE
AREA
1/8"

SADDLE
BOARD

FIG. 26

FIG 28
FOR ALL ROOFS

FIG. 27
FOR ALL SIDE WALLS
(SKIP WINDOWS & DOORS)

STEP 12. CHAMFERING THE PANEL

CUT A 45° ANGLE ON THE TOP AND BOTTOM EDGES OF THE PANEL (FIG. 29 and 30). MAKE IT ABOUT 3/8" WIDE. FOLLOW THE ARROWS IN FIG. 30 TO AVOID SPLITTING THE WOOD.

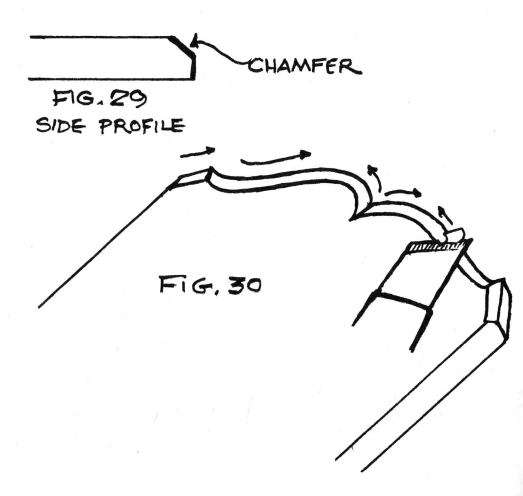

CHAMFER

FIG. 29
SIDE PROFILE

FIG. 30

STEP 13. LOCATING THE CLOCK WORKS

DRILL A ½" DIAMETER HOLE THROUGH THE CENTER
OF THE CLOCK FACE TO ACCOMMODATE A QUARTZ
MOVEMENT CLOCK AND DIAL STEM (SEE APPENDIX
FOR SUPPLIERS). THESE QUARTZ WORKS COME IN
DIFFERENT SIZES DEPENDING ON THE MANUFAC-
TURER, SO YOU WILL HAVE TO OBTAIN ONE FIRST
BEFORE YOU CAN RECESS AN AREA FOR IT ON THE
BACK. ALSO, MAKE SURE THE STEM IS LONG
ENOUGH TO GO THROUGH THE PANEL. PUT THE
STEM THROUGH THE HOLE AND SKETCH AROUND
THE MOVEMENT (FIG. 31).

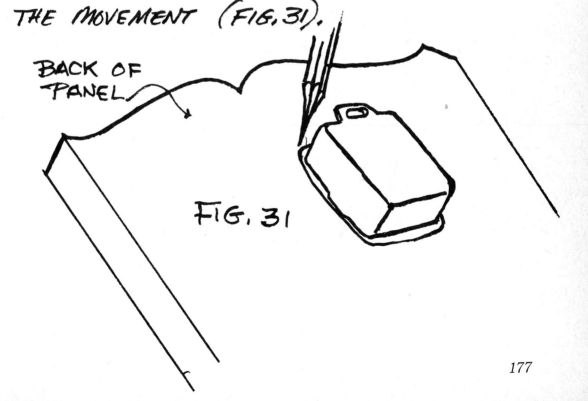

BACK OF
PANEL.

FIG. 31

STEP 14. MOUNTING THE WORKS

CUT STRAIGHT DOWN ALONG THE LINES MARKED IN STEP 13 WITH YOUR KNIFE AND REMOVE WOOD WITH A FISHTAIL GOUGE, MAKING THE AREA AS FLAT AS YOU CAN (FIGS. 32A and B). KEEP FITTING THE WORKS UNTIL THE DIAL STEM PROTRUDES AT LEAST 1/4" (FIG. 33). MEASURE HOW MUCH OF THE WORKS PROTRUDES ABOVE THE BACK OF THE PANEL AND MAKE BATTENS SLIGHTLY HIGHER THAN THAT MEASUREMENT (FIG. 32C). THESE CAN BE MADE FROM 3/4" THICK PINE 12" LONG. ROUND THE ENDS AND SCREW AND GLUE THEM TO THE BACK OF THE PANEL.

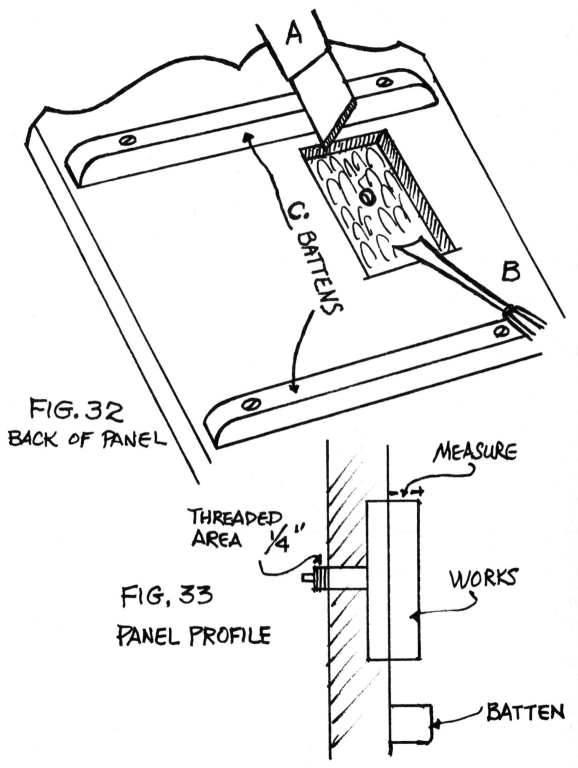

A

C. BATTENS

B

FIG. 32
BACK OF PANEL

MEASURE

THREADED
AREA ¼"

FIG. 33
PANEL PROFILE

WORKS

BATTEN

STEP 15 • MAKING THE KNICKKNACK SHELF

CUT OUT OF 3/4" THICK PINE TWO CORNER KNEES (FIG. 34 EXACT SIZE) FOR THE SHELF (FIG. 35). CUT ANOTHER PIECE OF 3/4" THICK PINE 3½" WIDE AND AS LONG AS THE PANEL IS WIDE. THIS WILL BE THE SHELF. HOLD IT IN PLACE WITH TWO SCREWS FROM THE BACK. NAIL AND GLUE THE KNEES INTO THE PANEL AND SHELF WITH 4d FINISH NAILS.

FIG. 34
NEED 2
3/4"
THICK

CORNER KNEES

CHAMFER

FIG. 35

STEP 16 · APPLYING A FINISH

STAIN THE ENTIRE PIECE EXCEPT FOR THE BUILD-
INGS WITH A GOLDEN OAK STAIN AND WIPE DRY.
USE A WALNUT STAIN FOR THE BUILDINGS. ALLOW
THE STAINS TO DRY OVERNIGHT AND GIVE THE
ENTIRE PIECE NO LESS THAN THREE COATS OF A
SATIN FINISH POLYURETHANE, SANDING LIGHTLY
BETWEEN COATS. NEXT, APPLY A SLOW-SET, GOLD-
LEAF SIZE TO THE DIAL POINTERS AND RIM AND
THEN GOLD LEAF (FIG. 36). OUTLINE THE POINTERS
AND THE TWO RIM LINES WITH BLACK. A TRUCK-
LETTERING QUILL (FIG. 37) WOULD WORK BEST
FOR THE OUTLINING. (SEE STEP 7 OF GAME BOARD)

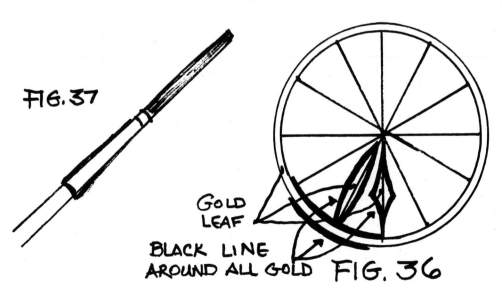

FIG. 37

GOLD
LEAF

BLACK LINE
AROUND ALL GOLD   FIG. 36

STEP 17 · PAINTING THE LIGHTHOUSE BUILDINGS

USE AN ENAMEL WHITE OR ANY OIL-BASED ENAMEL PAINT FOR THE TOWER (FIG. 38). PAINT ALL TRIM BOARDS, WINDOW AND DOOR FRAMES WHITE. PAINT THE CHIMNEY RED. PAINT DARK AREAS AT THE TOWER TOP A LIGHT PEA GREEN TO SIMULATE OLD COPPER. TRY MIXING A MEDIUM GREEN WITH WHITE AND A LITTLE YELLOW TO ACHIEVE OXIDIZED COPPER. PAINT THE TOWER WINDOWS SOLID BLACK. PAINT ALL WINDOW SASH WITH WHITE. ALSO, PAINT IN SASH BARS (MUNTINS AND MULLIONS) FIG. 39 - THE CLOCK IS NOW READY TO BE HUNG.

WHITE WINDOW & DOOR CASINGS

DARK AREAS ARE GREEN (TOWER TOP)

RED

WHITE TRIM BOARDS

WHITE

BLACK

FIG. 38

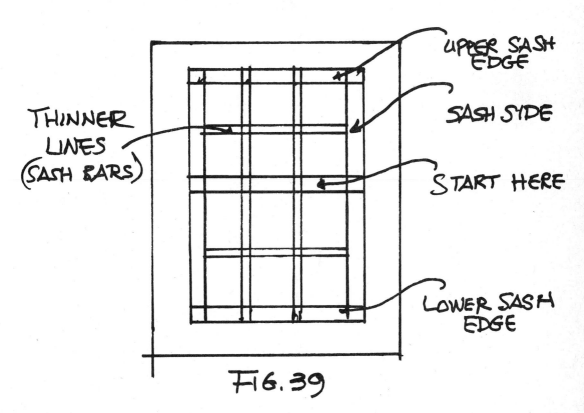

UPPER SASH EDGE

SASH SIDE

THINNER LINES (SASH BARS)

START HERE

LOWER SASH EDGE

FIG. 39

GAME BOARD

An attractive floor or table top game board

TOOLS NEEDED

FISHTAIL GOUGE ⌣

V PARTING TOOL V

McCARTHY KNIFE

JACKKNIFE

STEP 1 · MAKING THE BOARD AND LEGS

THIS BOARD MEASURES 16" SQUARE AND IS 2" THICK. YOU WILL PROBABLY HAVE TO GLUE UP TWO PIECES OF WOOD, A CLEAR WHITE PINE BEING THE BEST CHOICE BECAUSE IT IS EASY TO WORK WITH. FOR THE THICKNESS, YOU MAY FIND AT THE LUMBERYARD ONLY $1\frac{3}{4}$" OR 2" THICK PIECES AVAILABLE. GO WITH THE LATTER. AFTER GLUING AND CLAMPING, SMOOTH BOTH SIDES AND SAND. YOU CAN USE SCRAP ENDS FROM THE BOARD TO MAKE THE FOUR LEGS. BUT BE SURE TO FOLLOW THE GRAIN DIRECTION IN THE PATTERN FOR STRENGTH.

GAME BOARD PATTERN

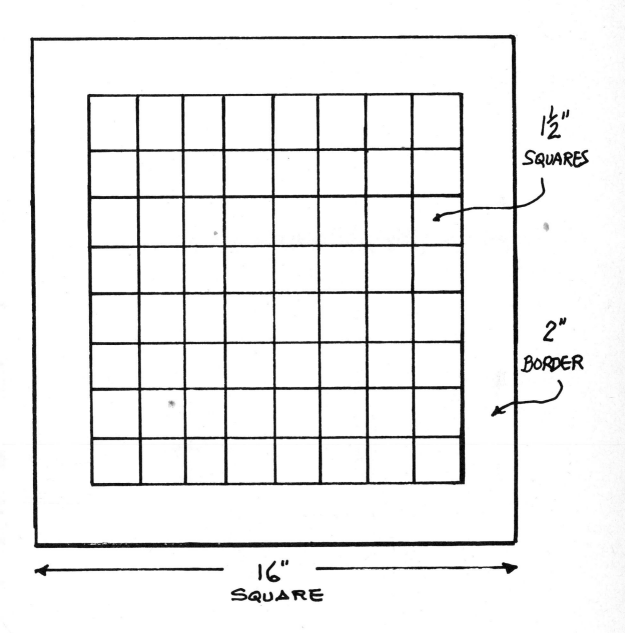

1½" SQUARES

2" BORDER

16" SQUARE

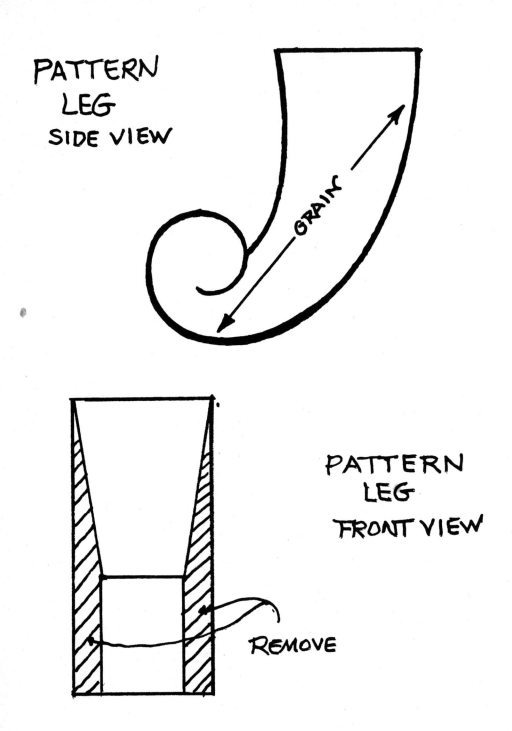

PATTERN
LEG
SIDE VIEW

GRAIN

PATTERN
LEG
FRONT VIEW

REMOVE

STEP 2. MAKING THE SQUARES

WITH THE McCARTHY KNIFE, MAKE A STRAIGHT—
DOWN CUT TO MARK ALL THE CROSS-GRAIN LINES
(FIGS. 1A AND 2A). DO NOT TRY TO CUT VERY DEEP
SINCE THIS IS ONLY A STOP CUT. NEXT, FORM A
SHALLOW 1/8" DEEP 'V' WITH THE KNIFE (FIGS.
1B AND 1C). TO MAKE THE LINES THAT GO WITH
THE GRAIN, USE THE KNIFE THE SAME WAY OR
USE A V PARTING TOOL (FIG. 2B). BE CAREFUL
NOT TO GET CAUGHT WITH CHANGES OF GRAIN
WITH THIS TOOL. IF SPLINTERING OR A RAG-
GED CUT OCCURS, GO IN THE OPPOSITE DIR-
ECTION WITH THE TOOL.

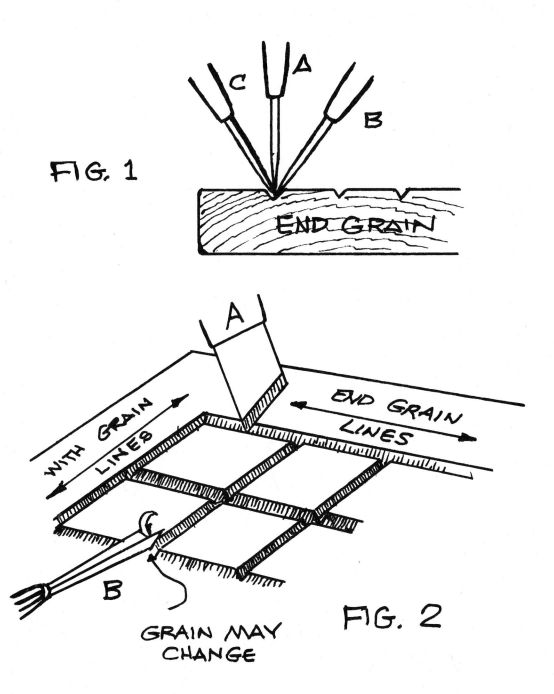

FIG. 1

C   A   B

END GRAIN

A

WITH GRAIN LINES

END GRAIN LINES

B

GRAIN MAY CHANGE

FIG. 2

STEP 3 · CLEANING UP AND ROUNDING EDGES

AFTER MAKING ALL THE INCISIONS FOR THE GAME BOARD, TAKE A PIECE OF SANDPAPER (100 TO 120 GRIT) AND FOLD IT INTO THIRDS (FIG. 3). SAND ALONG ALL GROOVES GOING BOTH WAYS AND SLIGHTLY ROUND ALL SHARP EDGES (FIG. 4A). DOING THIS WILL MAKE MOST OF THE CUTS UNIFORM. NEXT, MAKE A PAPER PATTERN OUT OF STIFF CARDBOARD AND SKETCH IN ONE ROUNDED CORNER ON THE CARD. TRANSFER THE PATTERN TO ALL THE CORNERS SO THEY ARE PERFECTLY EQUAL (FIG. 4B). USE A BAND-SAW TO MAKE THE CUTS. FINALLY, ROUND OVER ALL EDGES, TOP AND BOTTOM, SO THAT THEY ARE NOT SHARP (FIG. 4C).

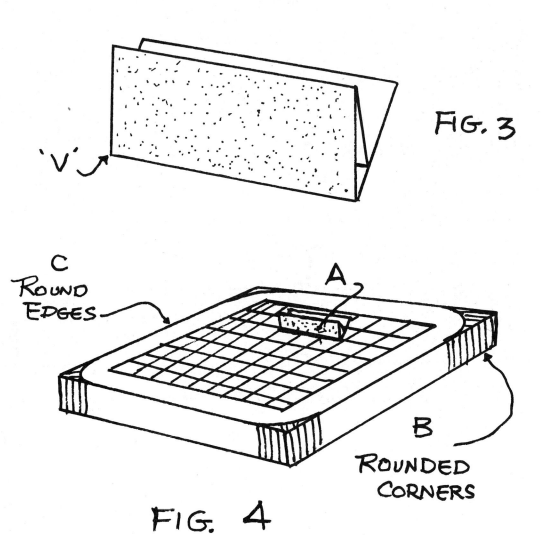

FIG. 3

C
ROUND
EDGES

A

B
ROUNDED
CORNERS

FIG. 4

STEP 4 · SHAPING THE LEGS

WORKING WITH THE GRAIN (FIG. 5A), CARVE THE BACK OF THE LEGS TO FORM A HALF-ROUND SHAPE (FIG. 6). CONTINUE THE CARVING ONTO THE BALL FOOT (FIG. 5B). A JACKKNIFE WOULD BE USEFUL HERE BECAUSE THIS IS SUCH SMALL WORK. ON THE FRONT OF EACH LEG, CARVE DOWN FROM THE TOP TO THE BALL AT AN ANGLE (FIG. 7A) ON BOTH SIDES. NEXT, ROUND THE BALL COMPLETELY INTO THE ANGLED CUTS (FIG. 7B).

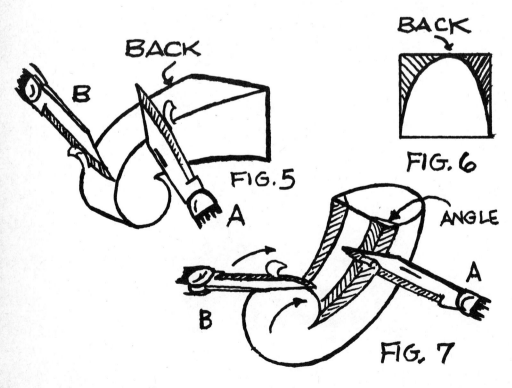

BACK

B

BACK

FIG. 5

A

FIG. 6

ANGLE

A

B

FIG. 7

STEP 5 · MAKING THE BALL FEET

SKETCH IN WITH A PENCIL THE HALF CIRCLES ON BOTH SIDES OF THE BALL (FIG. 8). USE A FISHTAIL GOUGE (SEE UNDER TOOLS NEEDED FOR THE SIZE) AND CUT STRAIGHT DOWN ON THE HALF CIRCLE (FIG. 8A). NEXT, CARVE AWAY WOOD AT AN ANGLE INTO THE BALL (FIG. 8B). YOU MAY HAVE TO USE ONLY PART OF THE EDGE OF THE GOUGE TO MAKE IT FIT THE TIGHTENED CIRCLE. BY REVERSING THE FISH-TAIL GOUGE, YOU CAN ROUND OVER THE OUT-SIDE OF THE BALL (FIG. 9).

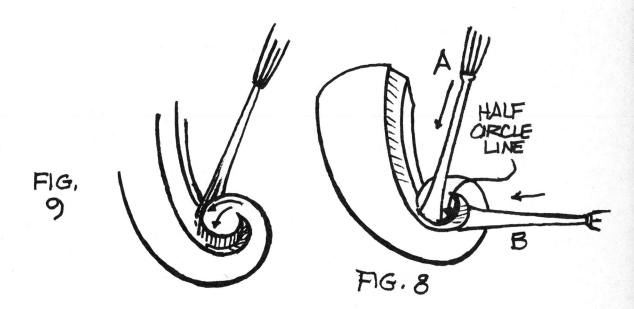

FIG. 9

A

HALF CIRCLE LINE

B

FIG. 8

STEP 6. SECURING THE LEGS

TO FASTEN THE LEGS TO THE BOTTOM OF THE BOARD, MAKE MARKS 2" IN FROM EACH CORNER FOR THEIR LOCATION (FIG. 10). WHAT WILL HOLD THE LEGS ARE 2" LONG DOUBLE-ENDED SCREWS $\frac{5}{32}$" OR $\frac{11}{64}$" IN DIAMETER (FIG. 11). DRILL 1" DEEP HOLES INTO THE BOARD AND INTO THE TOPS OF THE LEGS. INSERT THE SCREWS INTO THE BOARD FIRST AND TIGHTEN WITH PLIERS, PUT THE LEGS ON AND POSITION THEM SO THEY ARE POINTING TOWARD THE CORNERS (FIG. 12).

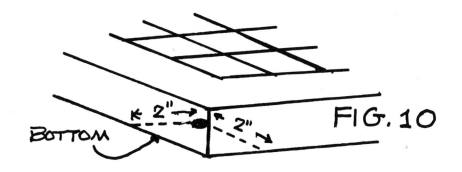

BOTTOM

2" 2"

FIG. 10

FIG. 11
DOUBLE
ENDED
SCREW

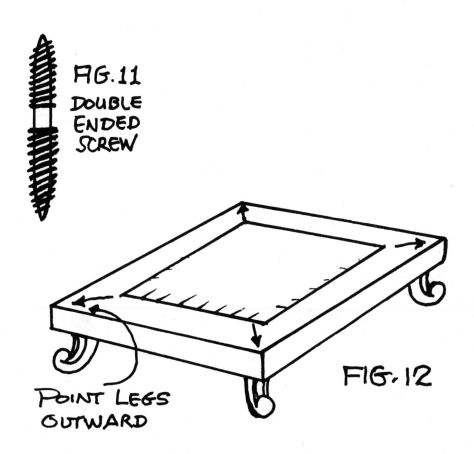

POINT LEGS
OUTWARD

FIG. 12

STEP 7 · FINISHING

NOW THAT THE GAME BOARD IS ASSEMBLED, YOU CAN START STAINING. FOR THE CHECKERBOARD FACE, YOU MIGHT TRY ALTERNATING LIGHT AND DARK STAINS SUCH AS MINWAX'S GOLDEN OAK AND JACOBEAN. THE EDGES, BORDER, AND LEGS ARE STAINED WITH A WALNUT COLOR. ALLOW TO DRY OVERNIGHT AND GIVE THE ENTIRE BOARD THREE COATS OF SATIN POLYURETHANE, SANDING LIGHTLY BETWEEN APPLICATIONS. FINALLY, PAINT THIN BLACK LINES INTO THE CARVED 'V'S TO ACCENT THE SQUARES. A #1 TRUCK-LETTERING QUILL WOULD BE USEFUL HERE (COMPARE THE WALL CLOCK PROJECT). FOR A FINAL TOUCH, GIVE ONLY THE CHECKERED PART OF THE PROJECT A COAT OF HIGH GLOSS POLYURETHANE.

Yacht "America"
Traditional
Half Ship Model

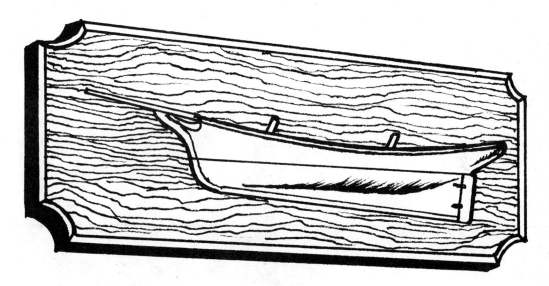

TOOLS NEEDED

McCARTHY KNIFE   JACKKNIFE

FISHTAIL GOUGE

Photo by Tad Goodale.

200

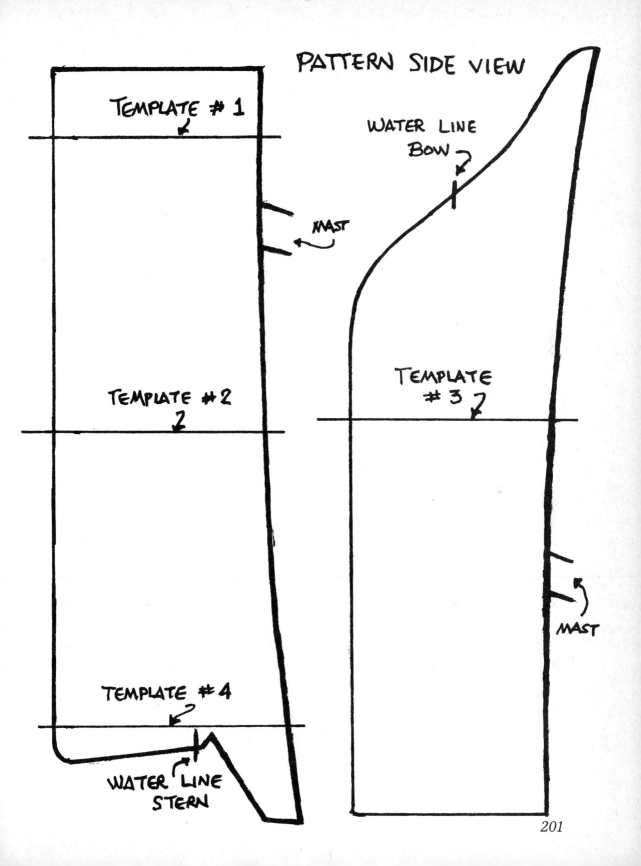

PATTERN SIDE VIEW

TEMPLATE # 1

WATER LINE
BOW

MAST

TEMPLATE # 2

TEMPLATE
3

MAST

TEMPLATE # 4

WATER LINE
STERN

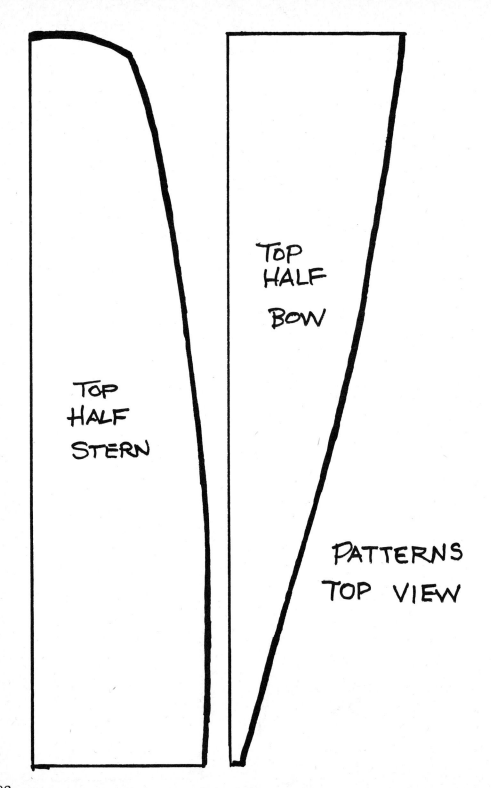

TOP HALF STERN

TOP HALF BOW

PATTERNS TOP VIEW

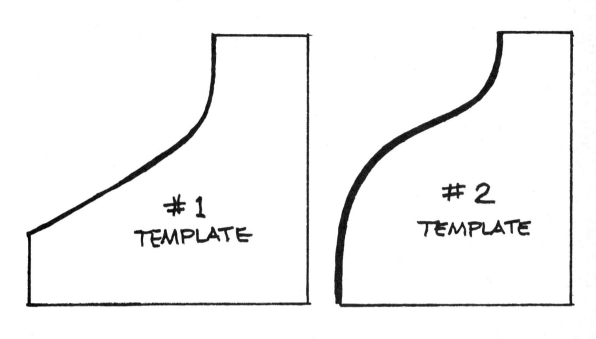

#1
TEMPLATE

#2
TEMPLATE

TEMPLATE PAGE

#3
TEMPLATE

#4
TEMPLATE

STEP 1 • TRANSFERRING THE PATTERNS

THE PATTERNS FOR THE SIDE AND TOP VIEWS ARE IN TWO SECTIONS BECAUSE, WHEN TOGETHER, THEY MAKE FOR A NICE HULL SIZE THAT IS OBVIOUSLY BIGGER THAN A PAGE IN THIS BOOK. TOGETHER ON A PIECE OF CARDBOARD, THEY ARE THEN TRANSFERRED TO A 2" THICK PIECE OF WOOD. USING KNOT-FREE EASTERN WHITE PINE WILL MAKE THE CARVING EASIER.

STEP 2. SECURING THE HULL

AFTER THE TOP AND SIDE VIEWS HAVE BEEN TRANSFERRED TO THE WOOD AND IT HAS BEEN BANDSAWED TO SHAPE, SECURE THE HULL TO A PIECE OF BACKBOARD. 3/4" PLYWOOD WOULD DO NICELY, AND IF YOU HOT MELT GLUE THE HULL TO THE PLYWOOD, YOU WILL BE CARVING IT WITH-OUT HAVING TO NAIL OR SCREW THE HULL TO THE PLYWOOD. YOU CAN THEN CLAMP THE PLYWOOD (FIG. 1). IF, AFTER CARVING, YOU HAVE TROUBLE PRYING THE HULL FREE, YOU CAN STICK THE BOARD INTO THE OVEN AND A LOW TEMPERATURE WILL LOOSEN THE GLUE.

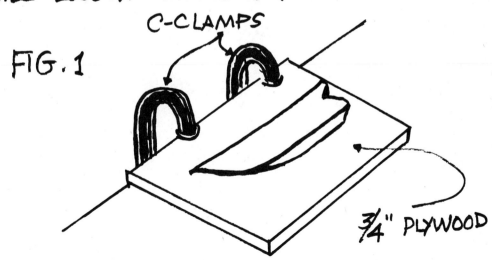

C-CLAMPS

FIG. 1

3/4" PLYWOOD

STEP 3. USING THE TEMPLATES FOR THE HULL MARK ON THE BACKBOARD WHERE THE TEMPLATE LINES ARE FOR THE MODEL (REFER TO THE PATTERN PAGE). THESE MODEL HULLS ARE FAIRLY EASY TO CARVE AS LONG AS YOU USE YOUR TEMPLATES CORRECTLY. SIMPLY LINE UP EACH TEMPLATE ON ITS LINE, STARTING WITH THE CENTER ONE, WHICH IS TEMPLATE #1. WITH THE McCARTHY KNIFE, CARVE AWAY THE HULL TO THE SHAPE OF EACH TEMPLATE (FIG. 2). THIS IS DONE BY EYEING UP THE HULL FROM THE ENDS UNTIL IT FITS THE TEMPLATE. SINCE THE CARVING IS THICKEST AT ITS CENTER, YOU CAN CARVE AWAY WOOD FROM THE BOW AND STERN AREAS AND REDUCE THEIR THICKNESSES.

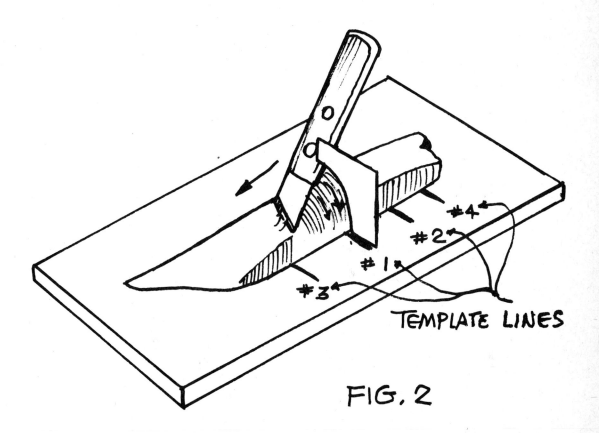

#4

#2

#1

#3

TEMPLATE LINES

FIG. 2

STEP 4 • SHAPING THE HULL (CONTINUED)

CONTINUE REMOVING WOOD ACCORDING TO HULL TEMPLATES #2 AND #3 (FIG. 3). THE WOOD AT THE STERN AND BOW WILL HAVE TO BE REMOVED AND SHAPED WITH A FISHTAIL GOUGE OR A HALF-ROUND GOUGE. CONTINUOUSLY TEST THE TEMPLATES' FIT SO YOU DON'T OVERCARVE ANY AREA. IF YOU RUB A LITTLE CHALK ON A TEMPLATE'S EDGE, YOU WILL BE BETTER ABLE THE SEE WHERE TO REMOVE WOOD SINCE A MARK IS LEFT.

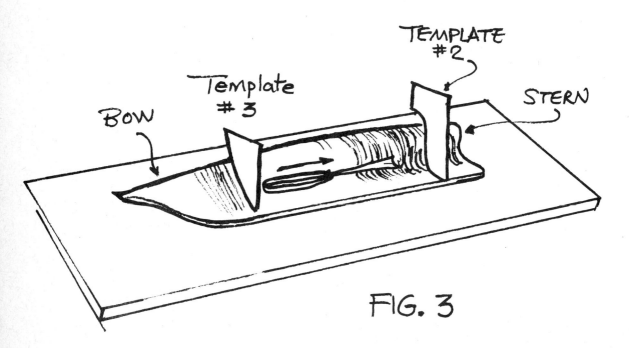

FIG. 3

STEP 5. FINISHING THE BOW AND STERN
TO COMPLETE SHAPING THESE AREAS, YOU WILL HAVE
TO USE A FISHTAIL GOUGE TO ACHIEVE A SLIGHTLY
CONCAVE AREA AT THE BOW AND STERN (FIGS. 4
AND 5). NOTE THE SHAPE AT THE BOW THAT, WHILE
BEING ROUNDED, CURVES INWARD AND FLATTENS OUT
FOR THE BOWSPRIT (FIG. 5).

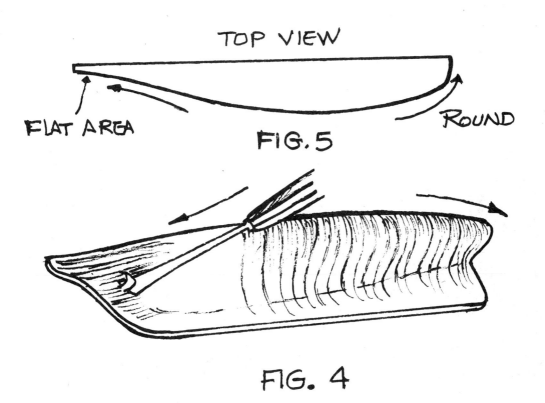

TOP VIEW

FLAT AREA

ROUND

FIG. 5

FIG. 4

STEP 6 - MAKING A KEEL

YOU WILL HAVE TO ADD A PIECE OF WOOD 1/4" x 3/8" x 16" (AT LEAST) ON THE BOTTOM OF THE HULL. THIS IS THE KEEL PLATE. PINE WOULD BE SUITABLE, BUT FOR CONTRAST, IF THE HULL IS NOT PAINTED, YOU MIGHT SELECT A DIFFERENT WOOD. USE THREE WIRE BRADS AND GLUE TO HOLD THE KEEL PLATE IN PLACE AND SET THE NAILS BELOW THE SURFACE WITH A NAIL SET AND HAMMER (FIG. 6). TRIM OFF THE EXCESS WOOD AFTER THE GLUE HAS DRIED AND CARVE THE HULL AND PLATE TOGETHER SO THAT THEIR SHAPES BLEND.

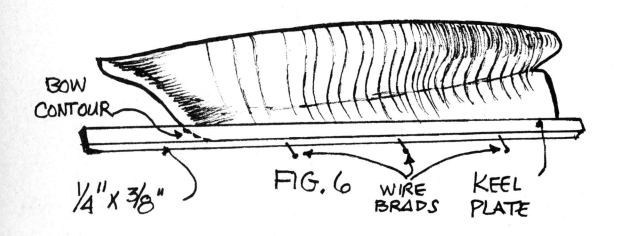

BOW CONTOUR

1/4" x 3/8"

FIG. 6   WIRE BRADS   KEEL PLATE

STEP 7• MAKING THE SHEAR AND WATERLINE

REFER TO THE SIDE PATTERNS FOR THE BOW AND STERN
WATERLINE MARKS. TO TRANSFER THESE ONTO THE HULL,
PLACE A PIECE OF WOOD THICKER THAN THE HULL ABOVE
IT (FIG. 7A). PLACE ANOTHER PIECE OF WOOD ON TOP
OF THAT AND ADJUST IT UNTIL IT IS OVER WHERE YOU
MARKED THE BOW AND STERN MARKS (FIG. 7B). LAY
THE SIDE OF A PENCIL FLAT AGAINST THE EDGE OF
THE BOARD (7C) AND SCRIBE A LINE ALONG THE
HULL. MAKE A SHALLOW 'V' CUT WITH THE
McCARTHY KNIFE OR V PARTING TOOL. NEXT,
SKETCH IN THE SHEAR LINE 1/4" DOWN FROM THE
TOP OF THE HULL FROM THE BOW TO THE STERN
(FIG. 8A). MAKE A STOP CUT ALONG THIS LINE
AND REDUCE IT SLIGHTLY FROM THE HULL (FIG. 9).
FINALLY, SKETCH IN THE TRAILBOARD (FIG. 8B)
AND CUT A SHALLOW 'V' AROUND IT. SAND ALL
THESE AREAS WITH A PIECE OF FINE SANDPAPER.

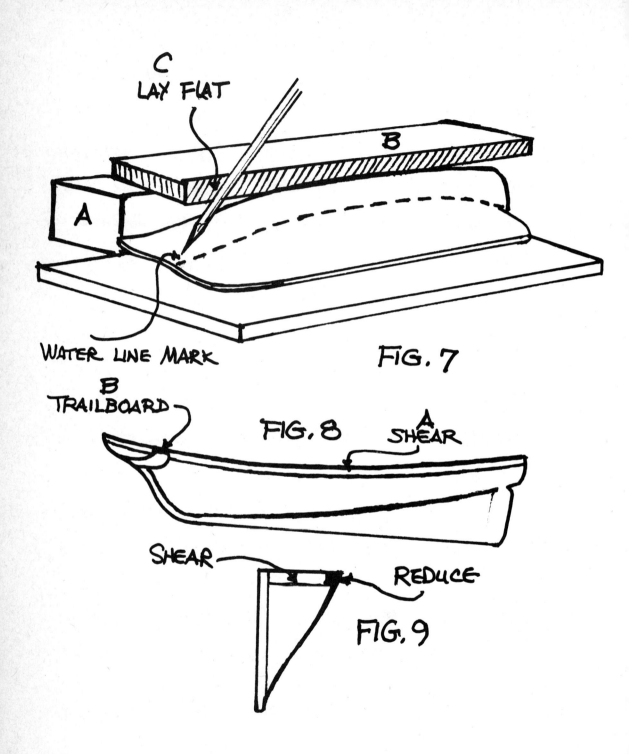

C
LAY FLAT

B

A

WATER LINE MARK

FIG. 7

B
TRAILBOARD

FIG. 8

A
SHEAR

SHEAR

REDUCE

FIG. 9

STEP 8. FINISHING TOUCHES

BECAUSE OF THE SIMPLICITY OF THIS HALF SHIP MODEL, YOU CAN APPLY DETAIL TO SOME AREAS SUCH AS THE BOWSPRIT, THE TRAILBOARD, AND THE RUDDER. USING THE ILLUSTRATION IN FIG 10A, SKETCH IN THE TRAILBOARD DESIGN. WITH THE POINT OF A JACKKNIFE, CUT STRAIGHT DOWN INTO ITS LEAF MOTIF. CUT STRAIGHT DOWN TO ACCENT THE INSIDE BORDER (FIG. 10B), THEN CUT A SHALLOW 'V' DOWN THE CENTER OF THE LEAVES (FIG. 10C). NEXT, CUT AWAY A NOTCH AT THE BOW (FIG. 10D) FOR THE BOWSPRIT. FOR THE RUDDER HARDWARE, REFER TO FIG. 11 AND SKETCH IT IN. WITH THE JACKKNIFE, CUT A SMALL 'V' AROUND THE PERIMETERS OF THESE SMALL RECTANGLES (FIG. 11A). CARVE A DEEPER V-LINE TO SEPARATE THE RUDDER FROM THE HULL (FIG. 11B).

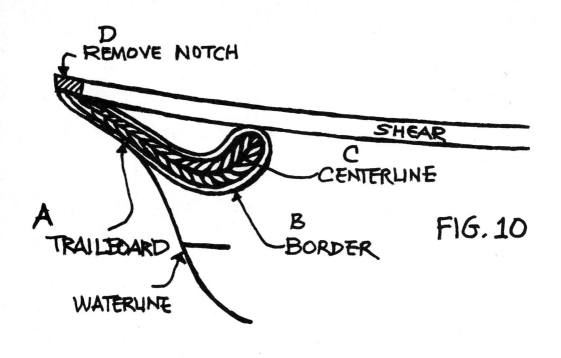

D REMOVE NOTCH

SHEAR

C CENTERLINE

A TRAILBOARD

WATERLINE

B BORDER

FIG. 10

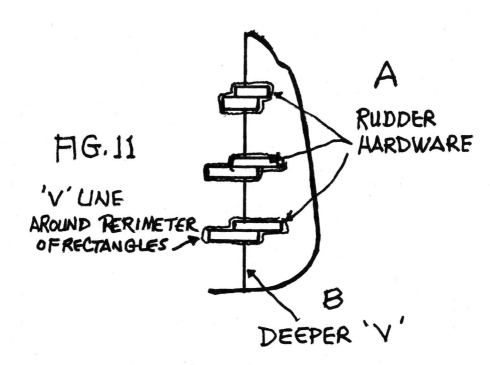

FIG. 11

'V' LINE
AROUND PERIMETER
OF RECTANGLES

A RUDDER HARDWARE

B
DEEPER 'V'

STEP 9. PREPARING A MOUNTING BOARD

CHOOSE A KNOT-FREE PIECE OF 3/4" EASTERN
WHITE PINE 11" x 22" AND NOTCH ITS CORNERS
(FIG. 12). THEN CHAMFER THE EDGES OF THE
BOARD-FOR CONTRAST TO THE FINISHED HULL.
STAIN THIS BOARD A GOLDEN OAK AND APPLY
THREE COATS OF A SATIN FINISH POLYURETHANE.
PAINT THE CHAMFERED EDGE A DULL BLACK
TO COINCIDE WITH A BLACK HULL.

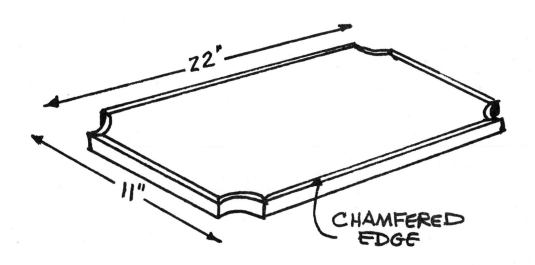

22"

11"

CHAMFERED
EDGE

FIG. 12

STEP 10. MAKING THE BOWSPRIT AND MASTS
FOR THE BOWSPRIT, SPLIT A 3" LONG, 1/4" DIAMETER
DOWEL DOWN ITS MIDDLE AND LOCATE IT AT THE
BOW (FIG.13). THE MASTS WILL NOT BE FULL ONES
BUT ONLY STUBS. EACH IS MADE FROM A 1 1/4"
LONG DOWEL 3/8" IN DIAMETER. THESE ARE TILTED
BACK AT AN ANGLE (FIG.14).

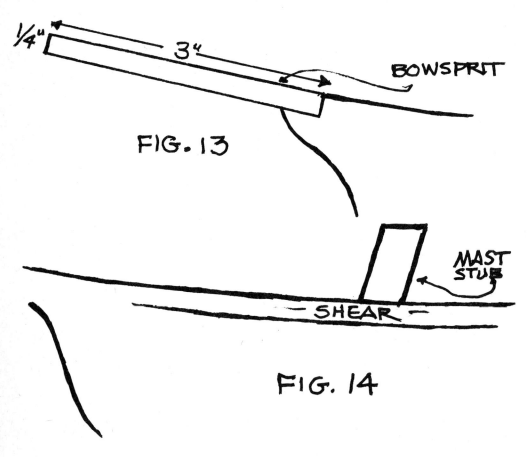

1/4"

3"

BOWSPRIT

FIG. 13

MAST STUB

SHEAR

FIG. 14

STEP 11· FINISHING

ONE WAY TO FINISH THE HULL IS TO GIVE IT JUST THREE COATS OF HIGH GLOSS POLYURETHANE FOR A SHINY FINISH. BUT IF YOU WANT TO PAINT IT, THE AMERICA'S COLORS ARE A GLOSS BLACK FOR THE HULL AND A DEEP RED OR MAROON FOR BELOW THE WATERLINE. PAINT THE BOWSPRIT AND HULL BLACK AND GOLD LEAF THE TRAILBOARD. AFTER THE RED OF THE RUDDER IS DRY, PAINT THE HARDWARE BLACK, REMOVE THE HULL FROM ITS BACKBOARD AND SECURE IT TO ITS NEW BOARD, MAKING SURE TO CENTER IT. YOU CAN USE THE WATERLINE AS A GUIDE. THEN GLUE THE MASTS AND BOWSPRIT IN PLACE.

Mallard Duck

DECORATIVE DECOY

TOOLS NEEDED

V PARTING TOOL V

HALF-ROUND GOUGE ⌣

JACKKNIFE

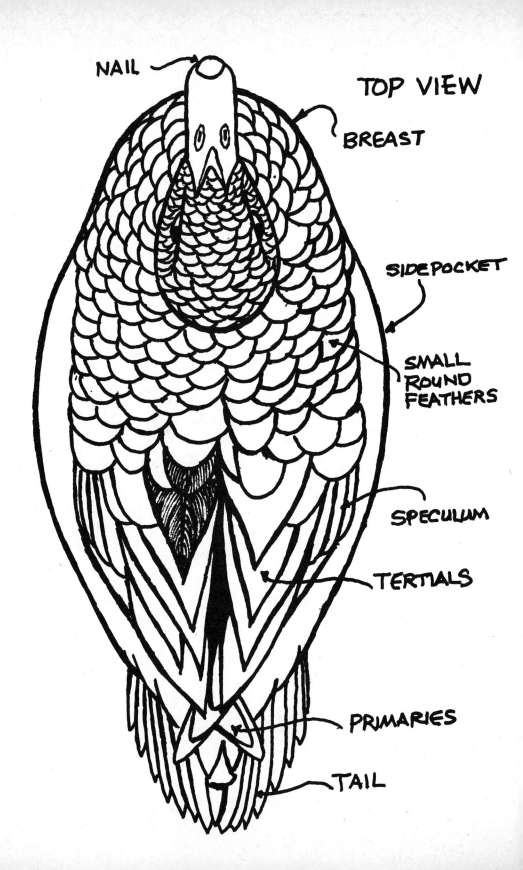

NAIL

TOP VIEW

BREAST

SIDEPOCKET

SMALL
ROUND
FEATHERS

SPECULUM

TERTIALS

PRIMARIES

TAIL

220

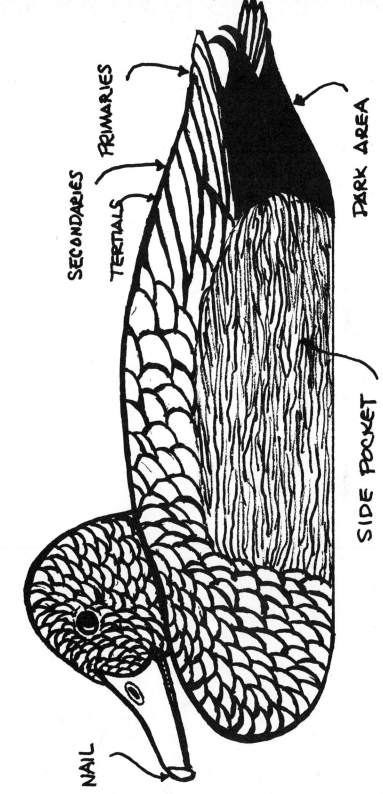

SIDE VIEW
FEATHER PATTERN

SECONDARIES

PRIMARIES

TERTIALS

DARK AREA

SIDE POCKET

NAIL

STEP 1. GLUING UP

THE BEST WOOD FOR THIS MALLARD WOULD BE BASS-WOOD. IT CARVES BEAUTIFULLY AND TAKES PAINT WELL. YOU CAN CARVE THIS BIRD ENTIRELY FROM ONE PIECE OF WOOD IF YOU CAN FIND 4"x4" STOCK. BUT IF NOT, YOU SHOULD GLUE UP TWO 2"x4" PIECES, USING A WATERED-DOWN SOLUTION OF WHITE GLUE SO A GLUE LINE DOES NOT SHOW.

STEP 2. BLOCKING OUT THE HEAD
USING A HALF-ROUND GOUGE, CARVE DOWN THE
SIDES OF THE NECK, EXPOSING THE HEAD. SEE FIGS.
1 AND 2 FOR TOOL USE AND WHAT WOOD TO
REMOVE.

REMOVE

TOP VIEW
FIG. 2

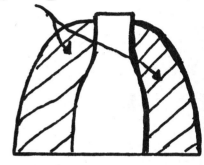

REMOVE

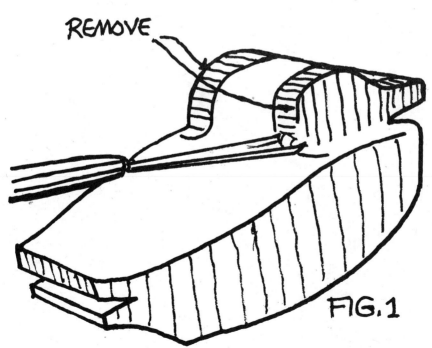

FIG. 1

STEP 3 · ROUNDING THE BODY AND BREAST

WITH A JACKKNIFE, CARVE FROM THE HIGHEST POINT ON THE BACK OF THE BODY TOWARD THE BREAST (FIG. 3). ROUND THE FRONT OF THE BREAST (FIG. 4) AND ROUND THE BODY SIDE TO SIDE (FIG. 5). DO NOT CUT INTO THE NECK AREA YET, BUT CONCENTRATE ON GIVING THE DUCK A GENERALLY ROUND SHAPE.

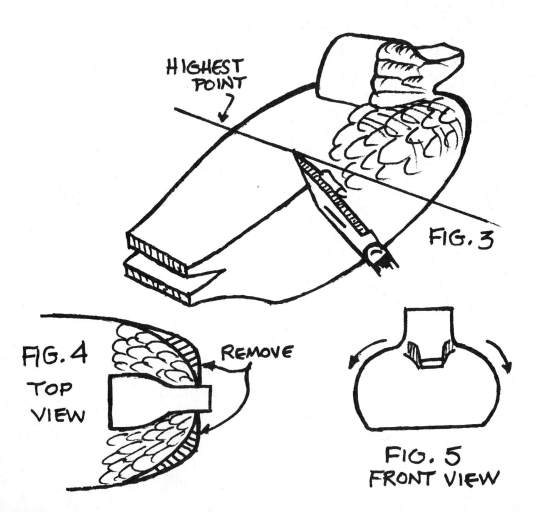

HIGHEST POINT

FIG. 3

FIG. 4
TOP VIEW

REMOVE

FIG. 5
FRONT VIEW

STEP 4. ROUNDING THE BODY (CONTINUED)
CARVE ALONG THE LOWER EDGE OF THE BODY (FIG. 6),
ROUNDING ALONG BOTH SIDES ONTO THE TAIL AREA.
CARVE AWAY WOOD FROM THE UNDERSIDE OF THE TAIL,
FOLLOWING AN ARC (FIG. 6 DARK LINE).

FIG. 6

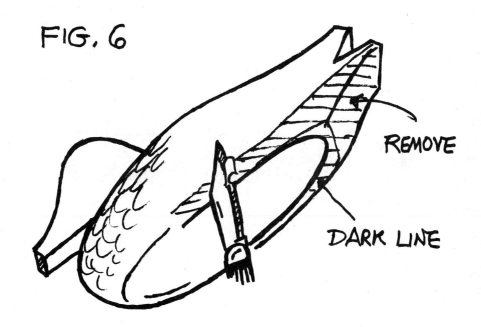

REMOVE

DARK LINE

STEP 5. ROUNDING THE BACK AND TAIL

CONTINUE ROUNDING THE BODY SIDES (FIG. 7). SHAPE
IN THE AREA WHERE THE FRONT AND BACK MEET
SO THAT THE BODY SIDES ARE BLENDED TOGETHER
SMOOTHLY. CONTINUE ROUNDING THE BODY ALONG
THE SIDES TOWARD THE UNDER PART OF THE TAIL. TO
SHAPE THE TAIL, FOLLOW THE ARROWS IN FIG. 8.
BE SURE TO CARVE AWAY ALL SAW MARKS.

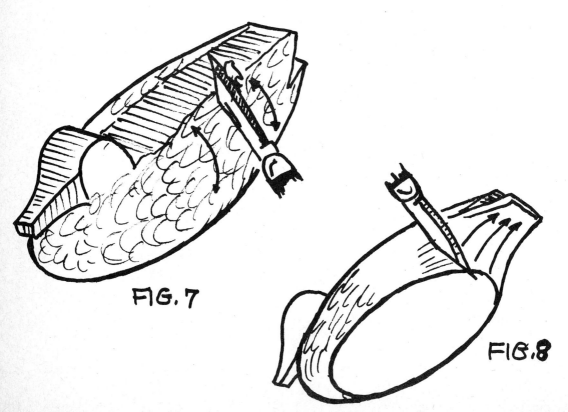

FIG. 7

FIG. 8

STEP 6. SHAPING THE SIDE POCKETS

USING THE PATTERN PAGE AS A GUIDE TO DRAW THE SIDE POCKET LINES, TAKE YOUR JACKKNIFE AND CARVE STRAIGHT DOWN INTO THOSE LINES WITH THE POINT (FIG. 9A) TO A DEPTH OF 1/4". REMOVE WOOD TO FORM A FLAT SHELF (FIG. 9B). THEN ROUND THE SIDE POCKETS AND BODY TO GIVE A FLUFFY APPEARANCE (FIGS. 9C AND 10). CONTINUE ROUNDING ONTO THE BACK FEATHERS AND TAIL AREA.

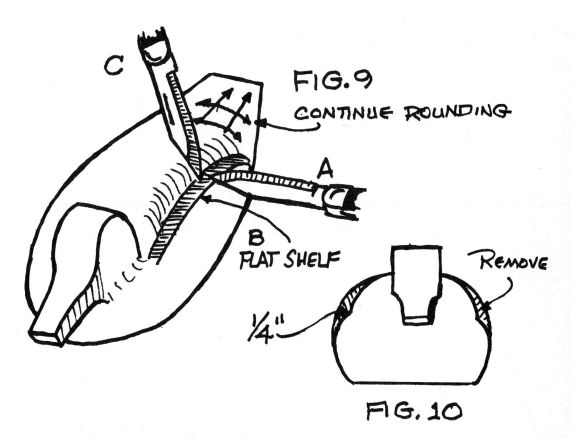

C

FIG. 9
CONTINUE ROUNDING

A

B
FLAT SHELF

1/4"

REMOVE

FIG. 10

STEP 7. SHAPING THE HEAD AND SHOULDERS

WITH THE JACKKNIFE, CARVE AWAY WOOD FROM BOTH SIDES OF THE HEAD DOWN TO THE BODY (FIG. 11A). WITH A HALF-ROUND GOUGE (SEE UNDER TOOLS NEEDED FOR SIZE), CARVE A GROOVE UP THE MIDDLE OF THE BACK, WIDENING THE GROOVE AT THE BASE OF THE HEAD (FIGS. 11B AND 12). CONTINUE ROUNDING THE BACK OF THE HEAD SHARPLY INTO THE BODY SO THAT THE BASE OF THE NECK IS A LITTLE LOWER THAN THE SHOULDERS (FIG. 13). ROUND THE SHOULDERS INTO THE HEAD BASE, THEN ROUND THE BACK INTO THE SHOULDER GROOVE (FIG. 11C).

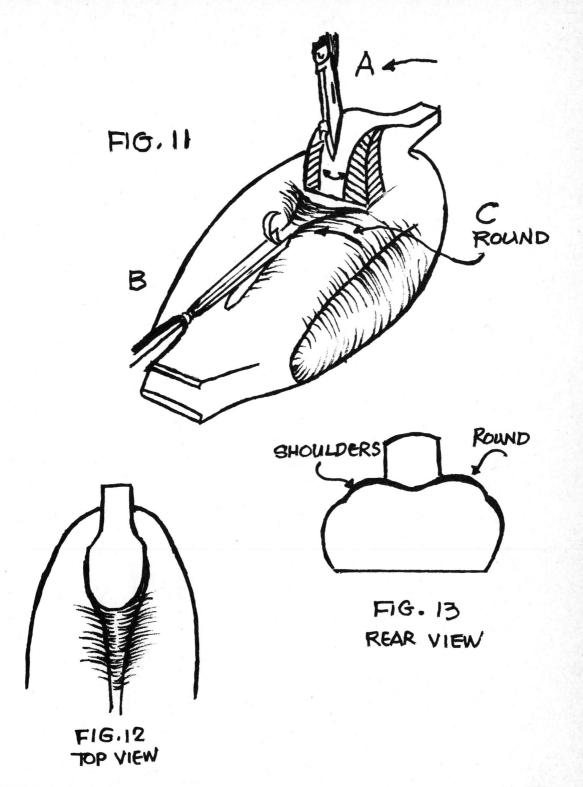

FIG. 11

A

B

C ROUND

SHOULDERS

ROUND

FIG. 13
REAR VIEW

FIG. 12
TOP VIEW

229

STEP 8· FORMING THE EYE SOCKETS
WITH THE JACKKNIFE, CARVE A CONCAVE AREA ON BOTH
SIDES OF THE HEAD DOWN ONTO THE BEAK (FIG. 14).
BE SURE BOTH EYE SOCKETS ARE EQUAL. ROUND ALL
SHARP EDGES INTO THE CHEEK AND HEAD AREAS
(FIG. 15). SAND THE HEAD AND EYE SOCKETS.

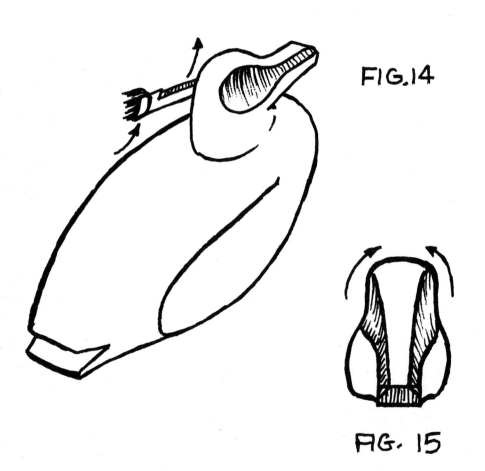

FIG. 14

FIG. 15

STEP 9. CARVING THE BILL

WHEN COMING TO THIS PART OF THE CARVING, IT IS ADVISABLE TO OBTAIN PHOTOS AND OTHER ILLUSTRATIONS FOR MORE ACCURACY.

BUT TO BEGIN, USE THE PATTERN PAGE SKETCHES AND DRAW IN THE BILL LINE, MAKING SURE BOTH SIDES ARE THE SAME (FIG. 16A). THEN, WITH THE POINT OF THE JACKKNIFE, MAKE A STRAIGHT-IN STOP CUT ALONG THE BILL LINE (FIG. 16B). LOWER THE BILL 1/16" FROM THE FACE AND CARVE DOWN ONTO THE BEAK, ROUNDING IT OVER SIDE TO SIDE (FIG. 16C). THEN ROUND THE BILL LINE BACK INTO THE BILL (FIG. 17A). THE END OF A DUCK'S BILL HAS A NAIL, A ROUND BUMP. DRAW THAT ON AND REMOVE WOOD AROUND IT, MAKING SURE TO KEEP THE END OF THE BILL ROUNDED AND NOT SQUARE (FIG. 17B).

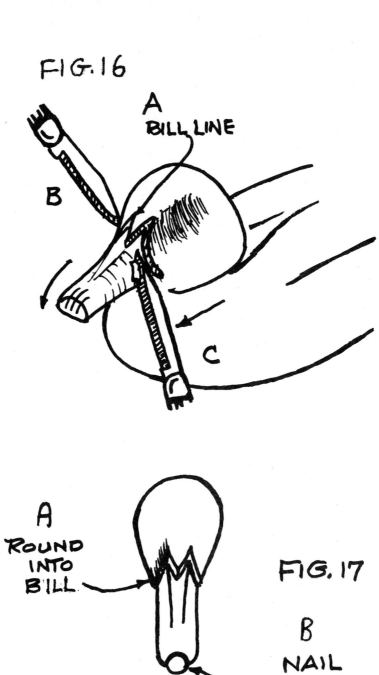

FIG.16

A
BILL LINE

B

C

A
ROUND
INTO
BILL

FIG. 17

B
NAIL

STEP 10 • FINISHING THE BILL

CARVE THE TOP OF THE BEAK TO THE SHAPE SHOWN IN FIG. 18. NOTICE THE BILL DOES NOT COME OUT IN A STRAIGHT LINE. CARVE THE SIDES OF THE BILL NEAR THE NOSTRILS FAIRLY FLAT, LEAVING A TRIANGULAR AREA (FIG. 19). CONTINUE CARVING DOWN THE BILL, ROUNDING AS YOU NEAR ITS END (FIG. 20). USING THE PATTERN, LOCATE THE NOSTRILS AND UPPER MANDIBLE (JAW) CREASE (FIG. 21). USE THE JACKKNIFE TO CUT STRAIGHT IN AROUND THE NOSTRILS AND CREASE AND REDUCE THE BILL SLIGHTLY BETWEEN THESE AREAS. CUT A DEEP 'V' FOR THE NOSTRIL HOLE (FIG. 21A) AND SAND THE AREA CAREFULLY.

FIG. 18

CURVES

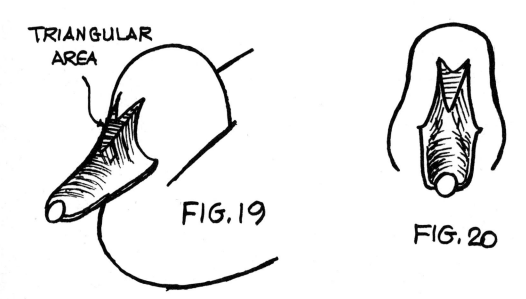

TRIANGULAR
AREA

FIG. 19

FIG. 20

FIG. 21

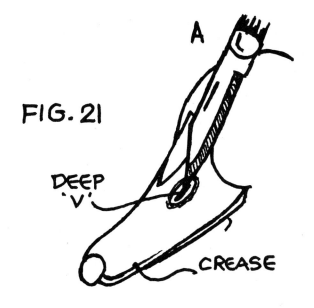

A

DEEP
'V'

CREASE

STEP 11 · SHAPING THE LOWER MANDIBLE

USING THE V PARTING TOOL, CUT TWO PARALLEL SLOTS ALONG THE UNDERSIDE OF THE BILL (FIG. 22A). THEN CUT A FINE V-SHAPED LINE ALONG BOTH SIDES TO SEPARATE THE UPPER AND LOWER MANDIBLES. ALSO BE AWARE THAT THE LOWER MANDIBLE FITS INTO THE UPPER MANDIBLE NEAR THE NAIL. REDUCE THAT AREA SLIGHTLY. WHERE THE BILL AND THE HEAD MEET, THE MANDIBLES CURVE UPWARD, FORMING A SMILE (FIG. 22B).

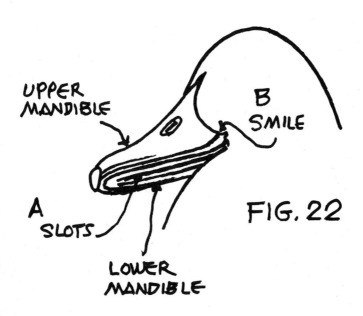

UPPER MANDIBLE

B SMILE

A SLOTS

FIG. 22

LOWER MANDIBLE

STEP 12· LOCATING THE EYES AND SETTING THEM
TO MAKE SURE YOU HAVE THE EYES OF THE DUCK BAL-
ANCED EVENLY ON BOTH SIDES OF THE HEAD, SKETCH
IN DOTTED LINES FROM THE NOSTRILS AND THEN OVER
THE TOP OF THE HEAD (FIG. 23). EYE UP THESE LINES
BY LOOKING AT THE HEAD STRAIGHT ON AND FROM
ABOVE. THE GLASS EYES YOU WILL NEED ARE BROWN
AND 7 MM. YOU WILL HAVE TO DRILL THE EYE HOLES
SLIGHTLY LARGER THAN 7MM. PACK THE HOLES WITH
ELMER'S CARPENTER'S WOOD FILL. MOST HARDWARE
STORES CARRY THIS. THEN CUT THE WIRES FROM THE
BACK OF THE EYES AND INSERT. KEEP WIPING AWAY
THE EXCESS FILLER THAT WILL SQUEEZE OUT SO YOU
CAN SEE THE EYE CENTERS TO ADJUST THEM. YOU
WILL WANT THE PUPILS TO LOOK A LITTLE MORE
FORWARD THAN STRAIGHT OUT FROM THE HEAD.
BE SURE EACH EYE IS SET IN AT THE SAME DEPTH
BY LOOKING STRAIGHT ON AT THE HEAD. THEN
PACK A LITTLE EXTRA FILLER AROUND THE EYES
AND LET DRY. ONCE IT HAS SET (AT LEAST AN
HOUR) USE A JACKKNIFE TO CARVE AWAY EXTRA→

STEP 12 · CONTINUED

FILLER (FIG. 24). YOU WANT TO FORM ALMOST A PER-
FECT CIRCLE WHILE KEEPING THE PUPIL CENTERED
AS YOU WORK ON EACH EYE. WITH THE V PARTING-
TOOL (FIG. 24A) FORM THE UPPER AND LOWER LIDS.
THESE MUST STICK OUT FROM THE HEAD A BIT.

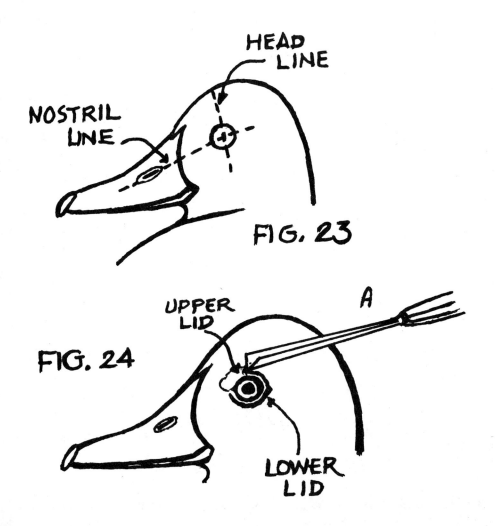

FIG. 23

FIG. 24

STEP 13. BURNING THE BACK FEATHERS

FOLLOWING THE BACK FEATHER PATTERN, SKETCH IN ALL BACK FEATHERS, INCLUDING THE PRIMARIES, (COMPARE FIG. 25). THESE CAN BE DEFINED WITH A BURNING TOOL WITH A SPEAR POINT TIP (FIG. 26A). THE DETAILER WAS USED FOR THIS (ADDRESS IN THE APPENDIX). WITH THE BURNING TOOL, START AT THE LAST ROW OF ROUNDED FEATHERS AND BURN PARALLEL LINES DOWN THE MIDDLE OF EACH, TAPERING THEM TO A POINT. THESE ARE QUILL LINES (FIG. 26B). FROM BOTH SIDES OF EACH QUILL, BURN IN THE BARB LINES WITH A SLIGHT ARC. THEN MAKE DARKER BURN LINES AT THE BASE OF EACH FEATHER (FIG. 26C). THESE HELP DEFINE THE CURVE OF THE ADJOINING FEATHER. BURN A FEW RANDOM AND DARKER BARB LINES INTO THE FEATHERS TO GIVE THE ILLUSION OF FEATHER SPLITS (FIG. 26D).

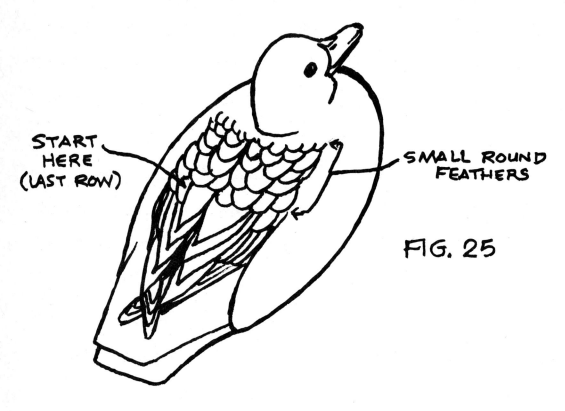

START HERE (LAST ROW)

SMALL ROUND FEATHERS

FIG. 25

FIG. 26

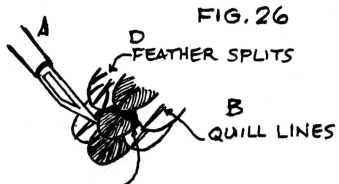

A

D FEATHER SPLITS

B QUILL LINES

C BURN DARKER HERE ALONG FEATHER BACK EDGE

STEP 14. SHAPING THE PRIMARIES

WITH THE POINT OF THE JACKKNIFE, CUT STRAIGHT DOWN ALONG THE OUTLINE OF THE PRIMARIES (FIG. 27A), CARVING TOWARD THE TAIL. BE CAREFUL NOT TO CUT INTO WHERE ONE SET OF PRIMARIES CROSSES ANOTHER. CARVE AWAY EXCESS WOOD, LOWERING THE AREA INTO THE TAIL PLATFORM (FIGS. 27 B AND C). DO NOT CARVE THIS AREA FLAT, BUT FOLLOW THE ACTUAL SHAPE OF THE BODY (FIG. 28). CARVE THE TAIL THIN, BUT GIVE IT A SLIGHT ARC, LEAVING THE BODY CENTER HEAVIER AND THE TAIL EDGES THIN (FIG. 29).

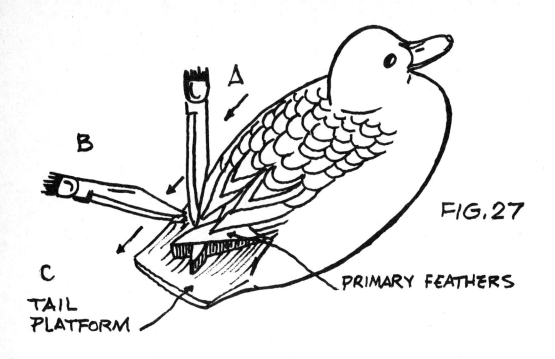

A

B

C

TAIL
PLATFORM

PRIMARY FEATHERS

FIG. 27

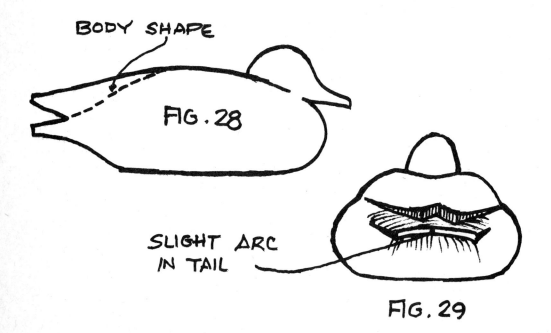

BODY SHAPE

FIG. 28

SLIGHT ARC
IN TAIL

FIG. 29

STEP 15 • SHAPING THE TERTIALS, SCAPULARS & SPECULUM

THE REMAINING BACK FEATHERS WILL BE SHAPED BY
CUTTING STRAIGHT IN WITH THE POINT OF THE JACKKNIFE
(FIG. 30A). LOWER EACH FEATHER SLIGHTLY, LAYERING
THEM LIKE SHINGLES (FIGS. 30B AND 31A). YOU WILL ALSO
WANT TO SHAPE EACH FEATHER OVER, FRONT TO BACK
AND SIDE TO SIDE, SO THAT EACH HAS A SLIGHT DOME
SHAPE (FIG. 31B). THE ONLY EXCEPTION TO THIS
ROUNDING ARE THE SPECULUM FEATHERS, AND
THESE ARE LAYERED FAIRLY FLAT (FIG. 31C).

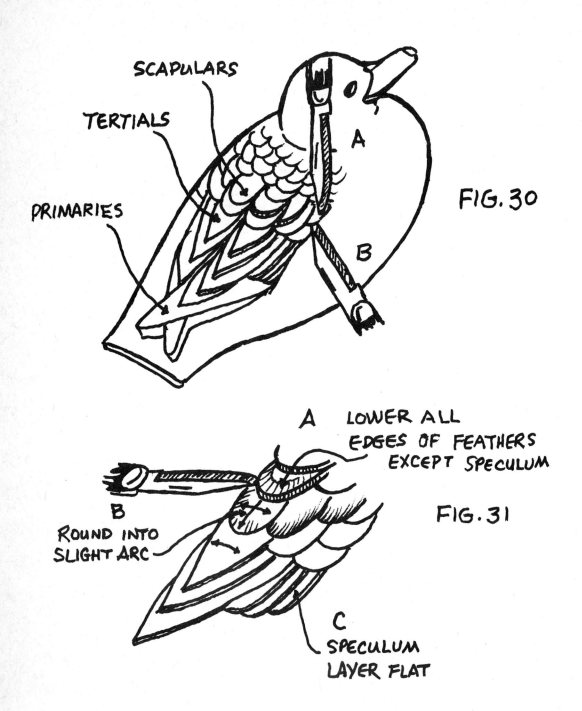

SCAPULARS

TERTIALS

PRIMARIES

A

B

FIG. 30

A LOWER ALL EDGES OF FEATHERS EXCEPT SPECULUM

B ROUND INTO SLIGHT ARC

FIG. 31

C SPECULUM LAYER FLAT

STEP 16 · UNDERCUTTING THE PRIMARIES

WITH THE POINT OF THE JACKKNIFE, GET IN UNDER THE PRIMARIES AND CUT AWAY WOOD A LITTLE AT A TIME (FIG. 32A). REMOVE WOOD FROM THE TOP OF THE TAIL BY CARVING INTO THE UNDERCUT (FIG. 32B) AND DOWN ONTO THE TAIL, THINNING THE AREA AS YOU GO (FIG. 33). AS YOU DO THIS, TRY TO LEAVE THE TAIL HIGH IN THE CENTER AND LOW ON BOTH SIDES, MAINTAINING THE ARC YOU WORKED ON IN A PREVIOUS STEP.

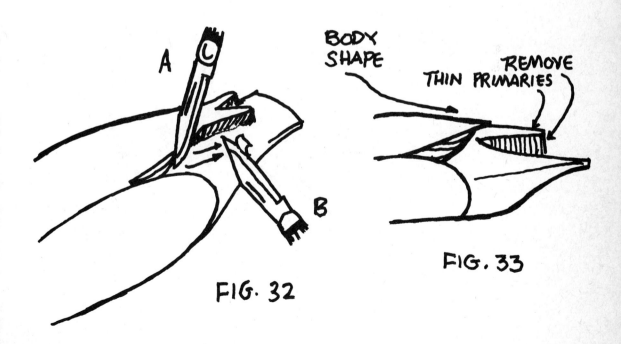

A

B

FIG. 32

BODY SHAPE

THIN

REMOVE PRIMARIES

FIG. 33

STEP 17. MORE WORK ON THE TAIL

THERE IS A SLIGHTLY CONCAVE AREA AT THE BASE OF THE TAIL (FIG. 34). THIS CAN BE RELIEVED WITH THE JACKKNIFE. THEN TRIM AWAY WOOD AT THE END OF THE TAIL TO GIVE IT A ROUNDED SHAPE (FIG. 35 A). THEN CUT STRAIGHT IN BETWEEN THE TERTIAL FEATHERS (FIG. 35B) AND REMOVE A SMALL AREA DOWN TO THE BODY. BE CAREFUL NOT TO CUT INTO THE PRIMARIES.

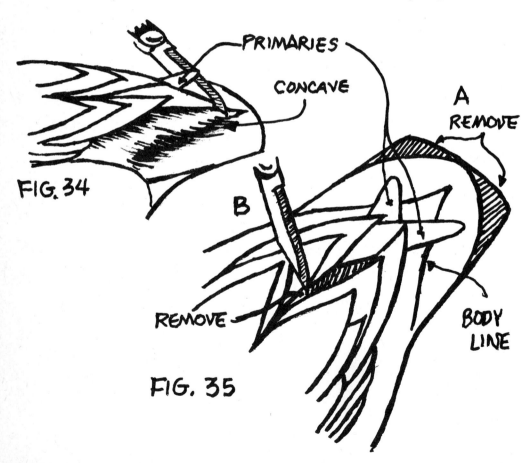

PRIMARIES

CONCAVE

FIG. 34

A
REMOVE

B

REMOVE

BODY LINE

FIG. 35

STEP 18 • FINISHING THE TAIL

USING THE PATTERN'S TOP VIEW OF THE DUCK, SKETCH IN THE TAIL FEATHERS AND CUT STRAIGHT DOWN WITH THE POINT OF THE JACKKNIFE (FIG. 36 A). LAYER THE FEATHERS FROM THE CENTER OF THE TAIL TOWARD BOTH SIDES (FIG. 36 B), BUT DO NOT CUT TOO DEEPLY SINCE YOU MAY BREAK THROUGH THE THIN AREAS. THEN MAKE NOTCHES BETWEEN THE FEATHER ENDS (FIG. 36 C).

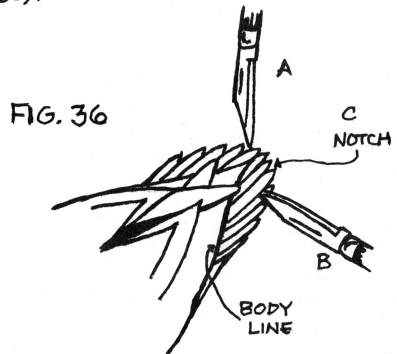

FIG. 36

A

C NOTCH

B

BODY LINE

STEP 19. MAKING THE HEAD AND BREAST FEATHERS

SKETCH IN ALL HEAD AND BREAST FEATHERS BY FOLLOW-
ING THE PATTERN. START AT THE BILL AND CHEEKS AND
SKETCH IN THE FEATHERS UP AND OVER THE HEAD ONTO
THE BACK OF THE NECK, IMPROVISING ON THE SIZES AS
YOU NEAR THE BASE OF THE NECK (SEE FIG. 37 ARROW
DIRECTIONS). FOR THE BREAST FEATHERS, START UNDER
THE BILL, SKETCHING TOWARD THE SIDE POCKETS, BUT
DO NOT DO FEATHERS ON THE SIDES. BURN ALL FEATHERS
AS YOU DID IN STEP 13.

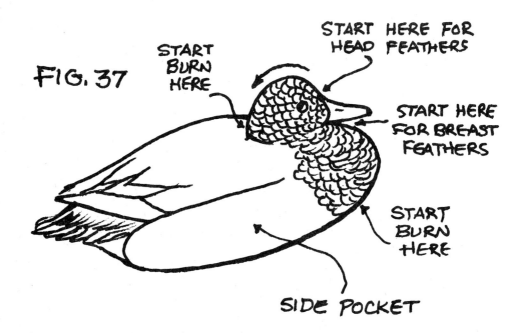

FIG. 37

START BURN HERE

START HERE FOR HEAD FEATHERS

START HERE FOR BREAST FEATHERS

START BURN HERE

SIDE POCKET

STEP 20 · FILLING IN THE SIDE POCKETS

FROM WHERE THE BREAST FEATHERS STOP ON THE SIDES AND WHERE THE SIDE POCKETS START, THERE WILL BE NO FEATHER PATTERN. INSTEAD, WITH THE BURNING TOOL, YOU WILL BURN A SERIES OF IRREGULAR, PARALLEL LINES, STAGGERING THEM ALONG THE SIDES (FIG. 38A). THESE WILL THEN BE FILLED IN WITH LINES BURNED AS CLOSELY AS YOU CAN GET THEM (FIG. 38B). FOLLOWING THE IRREGULAR LINES, GIVE THESE NEW LINES A WAVY PATTERN, BURNING COMPLETELY ALL THE EXPOSED WOOD.

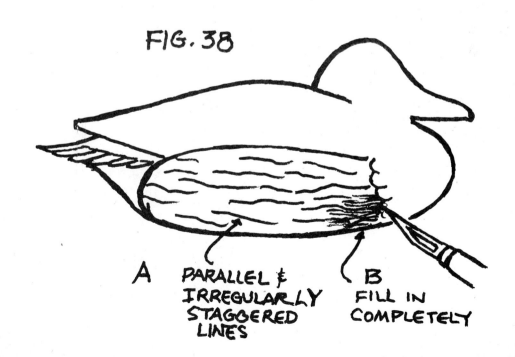

FIG. 38

A PARALLEL & IRREGULARLY STAGGERED LINES

B FILL IN COMPLETELY

STEP 21. FINAL BURNING

AS YOU DID IN THE PREVIOUS STEP, BURN IN UNDER THE TAIL (FIG. 39A). DO THE SAME FOR THE TERTIALS, SCAPULARS, SPECULUM, AND TAIL FEATHERS. (REFER TO FIG. 26). YOU CAN ALSO BURN UNDERNEATH THE TAIL FEATHERS BY FOLLOWING THE NOTCHED ENDS TO GIVE A FULL FEATHER DETAIL ON BOTH SIDES. REFER TO FIGS. 39 B AND 40. SKETCH IN PRIMARY PATTERN AND BURN AS YOU DID FOR TERTIALS.

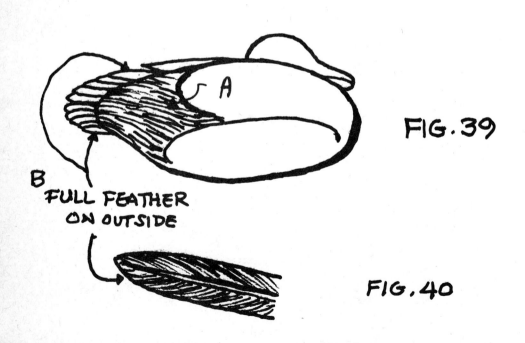

A

FIG. 39

B
FULL FEATHER
ON OUTSIDE

FIG. 40

STEP 22· FINISHING TOUCHES

WITH THE BURNING TOOL, BURN A V-SHAPED HOLE INTO THE CENTERS OF THE NOSTRILS, MAKING SURE BOTH SIDES ARE EQUAL IN SIZE (FIG. 41A). ALSO, BURN A SHARP LINE ALONG THE SIDES OF THE BILL TO SEPARATE THE UPPER AND LOWER MAN- DIBLES (FIG. 41B). BURN SMALL VERTICAL LINES AS CLOSE TOGETHER AS POSSIBLE TO FORM THE TEETH ON THE LOWER MANDIBLE (FIG. 41C).

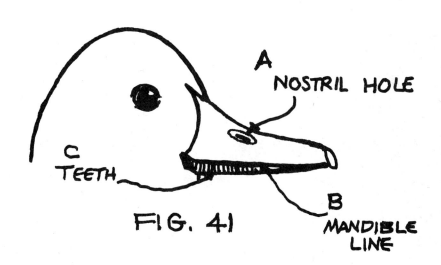

A NOSTRIL HOLE

C TEETH

B MANDIBLE LINE

FIG. 41

251

STEP 23 · PAINTING THE MALLARD

THIS DUCK WAS PAINTED WITH UNIVERSAL TINTING COLORS AND A FLAT WHITE (INTERIOR HOUSE PAINT) AND FLAT BLACK. START WITH A DIME-SIZED BLOB OF THALO GREEN ON YOUR PALETTE AND THIN TO A CONSISTENCY OF STAIN WITH TURPENTINE. DO THE HEAD WITH THIS THIN GREEN (FIG. 42). USE THE SAME PROCEDURE, BUT THIS TIME WITH THALO BLUE FOR THE SPECULUM FEATHERS. THE BREAST FEATHERS ARE DONE WITH A THINNED-DOWN BURNT SIENNA. FLAT BLACK IS THEN APPLIED UNDER THE WING TIPS AND THE REAR UNDERSIDE UP TO THE TAIL FEATHERS, BUT DO NOT PAINT THESE YET. PAINT THE SIDE POCKETS AND TAIL FEATHERS WHITE, DEFINING THE EDGES. YOU MAY HAVE TO APPLY TWO OR MORE COATS TO GET THE RIGHT COVERAGE. RAW UMBER, THINNED DOWN, IS THEN APPLIED TO THE PRIMARY FEATHERS. THE SCAPULARS ARE DONE WITH A WHITE AND RAW UMBER MIX TO CREATE A SOFT BEIGE. THE SPECULUM FEATHERS ARE NEXT (FIG. 43), WITH A WHITE LINE AT THE BEGINNING AND END OF →

STEP 23 • CONTINUED

EACH FEATHER, THEN A THIN BLACK LINE ON THE INSIDE OF THE WHITE LINES. GREEN ENAMEL OR ACRYLIC IS THEN APPLIED AROUND THE EYES TO PROPERLY COVER THE WOOD FILLER LEFT FROM A PREVIOUS STEP (FIG. 42). THE BILL IS DONE WITH A MIX OF ONE PART SATIN FINISH POLYURETHANE TO ONE PART YELLOW WITH A TOUCH OF RAW UMBER MIXED IN. DON'T FORGET TO PAINT THE UNDERSIDE OF THE BILL. FOR THE NAIL, USE A MIX OF BLACK AND RAW UMBER.

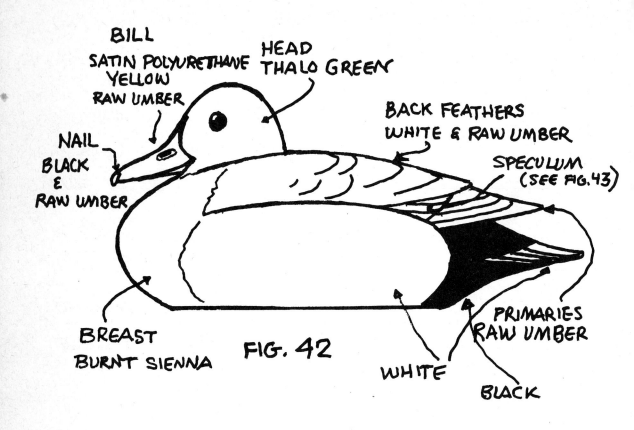

BILL
SATIN POLYURETHANE
YELLOW
RAW UMBER

HEAD
THALO GREEN

NAIL
BLACK
&
RAW UMBER

BACK FEATHERS
WHITE & RAW UMBER

SPECULUM
(SEE FIG. 43)

BREAST
BURNT SIENNA

FIG. 42

WHITE

PRIMARIES
RAW UMBER

BLACK

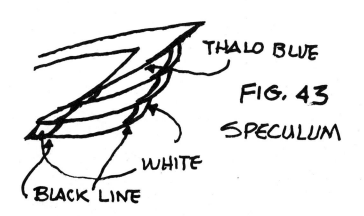

THALO BLUE

FIG. 43
SPECULUM

WHITE

BLACK LINE

STEP 24. CURLED TAIL FEATHERS & FINISHING TOUCHES
TO MAKE THE MALLARD'S DISTINCTIVE TURNED-UP PAIR
OF TAIL FEATHERS, GET A PIECE OF WOOD SUCH AS PINE
AND, WITH A JACKKNIFE, SLICE OFF SLIVERS WITH THE
GRAIN (SEE FIG. 44 FOR SHAPE). THESE SHOULD CURL
NATURALLY. CUT AN INDENTATION WITH THE JACKKNIFE
ABOUT 1" IN FROM THE END OF THE TAIL FEATHERS.
INSERT THESE TAIL FEATHERS WITH A DAB OF GLUE
INTO THE INDENTATIONS. (SEE FIG. 45 FOR LOCATIONS)
NOTE THAT ONE IS BEHIND THE OTHER. PAINT THESE
BLACK.

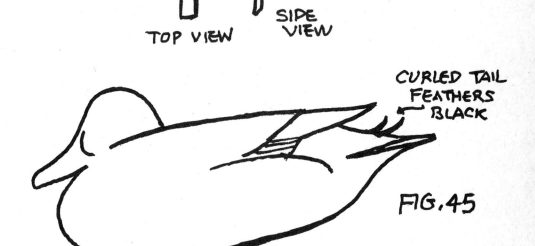

FIG. 44

TOP VIEW

SIDE VIEW

CURLED TAIL
FEATHERS
BLACK

FIG. 45